THE NARRATIVE LIFE

The Moral and Religious Thought of

Frederick Douglass

Scott C. Williamson

*Mercer
University
Press
Macon*

ISBN   0-86554-763-7 (hardback)
        0-86554-834-X (paperback)

MUP   H575
        P236

© 2002 Mercer University Press
6316 Peake Road
Macon, Georgia 31210-3960

First Edition.

Library of Congress Cataloging-in-Publication Data

CIP data are available from the Library of Congress

To my mother and father, Clarence and Odella Williamson,
and to my sister, Rachel Lynn Williamson

CONTENTS

PREFACE

Frederick Douglass is an arresting subject. Born into slavery in Talbot County on the Eastern Shore of Maryland, Douglass escaped his bonds in 1838 at the age of twenty. Within three years Douglass became a paid general agent of the Massachusetts Anti-Slavery Society. Within seven years, the nationally recognized abolitionist became a published author when he penned a narrative of his years as a slave. Within ten years, the internationally recognized lecturer and author owned a printing press and established a four-page weekly newspaper, *North Star*. By the time of his death in 1895, Frederick Douglass was one of the most prominent Americans of his generation. Among his accomplishments, in addition to his life's work as a lecturer, autobiographer, and editor, Douglass was a novelist, Republican presidential elector, recorder of deeds for the District of Columbia, and minister resident and counsel general to Haiti.

Frederick Douglass is remembered primarily for his fiery rhetoric as an abolitionist. Douglass's speeches, autobiographies, and editorials have been analyzed by historians, political scientists, literary critics, and more recently, by intellectual biographers in an effort to disclose his mind. Thanks to the work of these scholars, Douglass is recovered as an important thinker as well as a skilled rhetorician.

Douglass's moral and religious thought has received less sustained critical attention. The standard interpretation of Douglass as a religious figure is that his evangelical roots withered in the searing light of philosophic inquiry. The movement from evangelical Methodist to religious liberal is hailed as the definitive shift in Douglass's religious life, marking the transition from the immature to the mature Douglass.

There is certainly ample evidence to support this theory. Indeed, Douglass made reference to his own liberalism; a reference that underscored his commitment to think for himself and even to defy convention in matters of moral and religious concern. The image that I defend of Douglass's religious thought, however, is more complex than the one depicted by the standard interpretations. I will not argue the strong claim that Douglass was an acolyte or an evangelical disciple of Christ. Clearly he was not. But neither was Douglass merely an iconoclastic critic of Christian ecclesiology. Douglass railed against the church when he deemed that it sanctioned oppression or encouraged thoughtlessness in its adherents. He took the church to task for its hypocrisy, for an *otherworldliness* that anesthetized the faithful to injustice, and for an anti-intellectualism that made enemies of reason and piety.

The classification *religious liberal* succeeds in a broad way at framing these complaints with the church as well as the religious commitments from which they issued. Ultimately, however, the classification fails to make helpful distinctions along the axis of personal religious commitment. I am concerned, in other words, that the classification *religious liberal* under-reports Douglass's enduring fondness for what he called "the Christianity of Christ." For all of his alleged heresies, the sage of Anacosta loved to sing Christian hymns and found both edification and inspiration in public worship. The standard interpretation of Douglass as religious figure is not sensitive to the nuances of religious style nor to the gradations of religious commitment.

The standard interpretation of Douglass as moral agent reveals an ethical construct authorized by his humanitarianism. Here too, evidence abounds to make the case. I do not argue that Douglass's humanitarian zeal is over-reported. Rather, I think that his commitment to a moderate black nationalism is under-reported. The image of Douglass's moral life that I defend interweaves commitments to humanitarian reform and to black uplift that issue in a distinctive ethic of social justice.

In the course of rehearsing Douglass's moral and religious commitments, I portray a thinker who defies easy categorization. Descriptive terms such as *religious liberal* and *humanitarian* are helpful in that they locate Douglass within intellectual and social currents to which he was greatly indebted. There is an interpretive danger, however, to approaching Douglass from only this direction. Biographers can inadvertently emphasize only those broader features of thought and under-report other testimony, thereby formatting or masking the character they seek to reveal. To reduce this tendency in my report and to render a "thick" description of Douglass, I employ a narrative approach to my subject. That is to say, I approach Douglass by applying insights from narrative ethics. Two of these insights are central to my method: that character and circumstance render each other; and that we inherit and edit a moral world. We are shaped by moral systems even as we lend shape to them. Ever a social *me* and an agential *I*, the moral agent receives and recasts moral meaning in discrete social settings. Opposing world views were bequeathed to Douglass on the morality of slavery, nature of African humanity, and role of God vis-a-vis the "peculiar institution," to name a few, by the communities in which he participated. Douglass "edited" those views, he took sides, in consultation with the interpretive resources afforded him by his circumstance. In short, Douglass made use of what was available to him. His character, then, was informed as much by what was available to him, as by his reflection and deliberation.

The upshot of a narrative methodology for Douglass scholarship is that the story of Douglass's moral and religious thought begins with rich antecedents before his birth, and follows closely the episodes of his life. A compelling account of Douglass as thinker includes a sensitive account of his circumstances and a nuanced account of his character. Given my methodological commitments, I cannot hope to analyze every circumstance of Douglass's life in this volume. Seventy-seven years of history is not easily scrutinized. I focus my attention, therefore, on Douglass's moral and religious thought from his first days to the Civil War. I focus on these years for two reasons: to illumine the rich antecedents of his thought; and, based on these antecedents, to provide evidence for what I believe to be enduring moral and religious themes in Douglass's life. In my conclusion, I hold these themes in tension with the standard conclusions on Douglass's moral and religious thought.

1

THE EASTERN SHORE

INTRODUCTION

Beginning in slavery and continuing into what I am calling his period of maturity, Frederick Douglass filtered disparate moral, religious, and political elements through his intellect, imagination, and will to produce a syncretistic faith system. Douglass's faith, a discrete "way of knowing," held in tension his roles as an abolitionist, a Christian, an editor, an American, a black nationalist, an integrationist, a humanist, and a progressive social reformer.[1] His moral development was likewise richly informed from many schools of thought, owing in the majority to no one particular stream of moral discourse. It was most inspired by the

---

[1] "Faith" is distinguished from "belief." More than mere assent, "faith" is an ongoing activity in creating meaning. I am indebted to Wilfred Cantwell Smith, *Belief and History* (Charlottesville: University of Virginia Press, 1977) and *Faith and Belief* (Princeton NJ: Princeton University Press, 1979); James W. Fowler, *Stages of Faith: The Psychology of Human Development and the Quest for Meaning* (New York: Harper and Row, 1981); and James B. Hunt, "The Faith Journey of Frederick Douglass, 1818–1895," *Christian Scholar's Review*, 15:3, (March, 1986): 228–46.

objects of universal freedom and material equality, and underscored by those arguments that furthered these basic commitments.[2] His religion was grounded in neither dogma nor liturgy. Rather, it was set in the affirmation of its basic story, in its prophetic insights, and in its assurance of spiritual—if not also material—deliverance. His politics advanced strategies to realize public manifestations of the moral and religious antecedents given legitimacy within the faith system developed over time. In the years of his most significant work, from his first narrative through the end of the Civil War, Frederick Douglass appealed to God in defense of his politics and for its culmination in the abolition of slavery from the American scene in particular, and the western and African experience in general.

Douglass demonstrated that he had a conception of God as holy and revealed through his reliance upon biblical stories, metaphors, and parables. The language and symbols of Christianity provided Douglass with the vocabulary of his primary, or "first order," religious discourse.[3] Traditional Christian terms like "sin," and "judgment" are woven into the fabric of his early writings on slavery. Douglass's beliefs about God, and his appropriation of Christian discourse, helped him to make sense of his experiences in slavery and to articulate a vision of a more just society.

As he matured, Douglass used more abstract and philosophical language to express beliefs about God. For this "second order" conceptual and interpretive language, Douglass borrowed from a strain of religious liberalism he encountered through Garrisonian abolitionists. Instead of moving towards greater philosophical clarity by appealing consistently to either the primary or secondary modes of religious discourse, Douglass demonstrated the complexity of his religious thought by contemporaneous use of traditional Christian referents (such as

---

[2] "Material" equality has an economic connotation that makes it more practical and meaningful when applied to the oppressed than the "idealistic" variant of equality that stresses equality of personhood or equality before God.

[3] James Livingston, *Anatomy of the Sacred: An Introduction to Religion*, 2nd ed. (New York: Macmillan Publishing Company, 1993) 77.

biblical parables and metaphors), and of the more recent rationalist and deist language of New England Transcendentalism.

The relation of these two modes of discourse is no small problem for interpreters. Recent scholarship tends to support the theory that Douglass transformed from an evangelical Methodist to a religious liberal[4] in the period from his conversion at age thirteen to his tenure as an editor in the public print media. Even a cursory glance at Douglass's autobiographies provides ample evidence that his religion is seen most clearly through the interpretive lens of religious *erosion*. In other words, his greater dependence upon the authority of a personal God eroded over time. That is the key to understanding Douglass's faith.

The claim here is not that Douglass forswore earlier Christian convictions in favor of later non-Christian affirmations. Rather, Douglass's faith became one in which a religious dogma affirming the personal authority and imminence of God was increasingly muted. Some scholars, such as Waldo Martin, depict a fairly thorough process of transformation through erosion. Others, such as David Blight, offer a more subtle and modest evaluation of the process. Blight makes an important contribution to what I refer to as the "erosion theory," that Douglass did not "push God offstage." I share Blight's read. Douglass never became so liberal in religious beliefs that he dispensed entirely with the image of a

---

[4] In claiming that Douglass was a liberal, scholars locate him within the nineteenth century movement known as Liberalism, a movement that fostered political, economic, and religious theories. Politically, liberalism endorsed the autonomy of the individual and championed individual civil liberties. Economically, liberalism was committed to the individual's pursuit of wealth. It advocated the free market, the gold standard, and *laissez-faire* capitalism. In matters of religion, liberalism challenged orthodoxy. It emphasized the individual's free and active pursuit of new religious ideas, the centrality of ethics within Christian theology and ecclesiology, and it criticized dogmatic theology. For a helpful overview of Liberalism, refer to the American Heritage Dictionary, third edition. For a more thorough account of Protestant liberalism in the late eighteenth and early nineteenth centuries, refer to Reinhold Niebuhr, "The Blindness of Liberalism," *Radical Religion*, Autumn, 1936. The liberal code as Niebuhr describes it contains propositions that Douglass did not accept, such as the stupidity of warfare, but the code effectively captures the spirit of the movement in which Douglass flourished.

personal God or completely disavowed the power of that image in his own religious experience.

An alternate portrayal of Douglass's evolving faith system is based on the developmental theories of Erikson, Piaget, Kohlberg, and theologian-psychologist James Fowler. Applying Fowler's model of "faith development," James Hunt argues that Douglass's faith journey underwent a process of change.[5] Instead of *erosion*, Hunt favors faith *development*[6] as a master interpretive key to Douglass's religious life. Though the construct is different, the upshot is largely the same. Hunt outlines three "stages" in Douglass's change from evangelical Methodist to classic religious liberal: Methodism, Abolitionism, Liberalism.[7]

Biographers are correct to pursue a systematic framework with which to interpret the different ways in which Douglass expressed his faith. The theories of religious erosion and faith development can help us understand Douglass. I have two concerns, however, regarding how these various approaches seek to define Douglass's faith and its expression. One concern is that theorists mistakenly endeavor to resolve the tension in Douglass's religious outlook—that between traditional Christian perspectives and the later classic liberal points of view. It is a tension that informs the depth of Douglass's faith and need not be artificially "resolved" by asserting an absolutist view of religious authority in Douglass's life. The other concern is that the term "liberalism," used as an umbrella term to define the scope and categorize the content of Douglass's religious thought, illuminates the changes that Douglass underwent but obscures those theological commitments that occasioned his broad-mindedness. Theorists gain conceptual clarity by interpreting Douglass in light of his liberalism, but they under-report the rich antecedents that culminated in his progressive views. Douglass's life was not a smooth process of development on an even keel. In the pages that follow, I will offer an alternate framework for understanding

---

[5] Hunt, "Faith Journey of Frederick Douglass," 230.
[6] Italics mine.
[7] Hunt, "Faith Journey of Frederick Douglass," 244.

Douglass; one that portrays a man who held disparate interpretive mediums in dialectical tension. It is a significant challenge to fully portray the character of Douglass's religious faith. How, for example, does one deduce the religious creeds Douglass held in the absence of any formal credo? By analyzing Douglass's appeals to religious language and thought, however, it is possible to organize a rudimentary model of his creedal system.

It is helpful to come to terms with whether Douglass had an intrinsic or extrinsic orientation to Christianity. On Gordon Allport's account, persons with an extrinsic orientation to religion, "are disposed to use religion for their own ends.... may find religion useful in a variety of ways, to provide security and solace, sociability and distraction, status and self-justification."[8] Persons with an intrinsic orientation to religion, "find their master motive in religion....Having embraced a creed the individual endeavors to internalize it and follow it fully. It is in this sense that he lives his religion."[9]

At times Douglass biographers make the case that he had an extrinsic orientation to religion. They argue that Douglass used religion to advance more central concerns, namely abolition or related social reforms. This position is merited. Douglass commented in his first narrative (1845) that after suffering a cruel beating by an overseer in 1834 his hands were no longer tied by his religion. He did not renounce his faith, neither did he renounce the use of violence in his bid for fair treatment. According to an extrinsic interpretation, religion provided at best a justification for the work of abolition. That is to say, Douglass intended to fight for freedom with or without religious sanction, but preferably with it.

A strong case can be made, however, that Douglass had an intrinsic orientation to religion. He consistently criticized the slaveholding church for using religion to justify slavery. He also criticized the black church for using religion to advance an agenda of complacency, when religion properly interpreted required they fight for justice. He wrote that he loved the religion of Christ, but

---

[8] Gordon Allport, quoted in Livingston, *Anatomy of the Sacred*, 37–38.
[9] Ibid., 38.

hated many of the selfish and oppressive social practices that bore Christ's name. By an intrinsic account, Douglass's religion adhered to a "master motive" and embraced a creed. His master motive was the "pure, peaceable and impartial Christianity of Christ." Making social reform (including abolition) a reality was his primary creedal principle. The work of abolition, then, served as the proper embodiment of "pure" Christianity and not in the stead of Christianity. Moral arguments for abolition underscored essentially religious estimates of freedom and justice.

Even during times of religious doubt, Douglass held fast to his belief in a personal God. He failed at times of distress to understand how God was active in the world, but even here did not push God offstage. He speculated at least once that God's domain was apart from the human domain.

Although his basic affirmation of the Christian story made Douglass a Christian, it is also possible to deduce a rudimentary creedal system from his writings and speeches. Douglass's creed during the antebellum years included: divine omnipotence and holiness; divine transcendence; divine immanence; belief that Scripture is God's revealed Word; belief in a hereafter; belief in God's assurance of salvation; belief in emancipation; belief in racial and gender equality; belief in social reform. Affirming the first six creedal principles without incorporating the latter three struck Douglass as a sham religion that sanctioned evil in the worship of God. His creed promoted social justice as an act of worship. The latter three principles comprised a faithful social witness to the first six.

Douglass's moral and religious beliefs, including his use of the Bible and the overall appropriation of the abolition movement's views, disclose an active and fertile mind. Douglass did more than simply mirror the important ideas of his era. He selected, revised, and transformed the episodes and intellectual currents that impinged upon him, and gained his own distinct voice in the process. Douglass was not simply a chronicler of events, neither was he merely a rhetorician. On the contrary, Douglass displayed originality in his moral and religious thought.

This was no small accomplishment for a self-schooled fugitive slave. Unlike white abolitionists of the time, Douglass was embedded within the media of overlapping and oppositional communities, one black and the other white. Where the media of those communities were dissimilar, Douglass made choices. Though he adopted the vocabulary of Northern, white intellectuals, he did so to articulate the patterns of ritual, myth, belief, and conduct endemic to black slaves. For example, in reasoning on the moral difference between "stealing" and "appropriating," Douglass elevated black experience above the prevailing normative moral language via the idiom of Northern white moralists. Douglass is most visible as an original thinker standing at the juncture between two dissimilar communities, two different ways of knowing. Though he was not a systematic thinker, Douglass integrated and applied narrative influences, intellectual currents, and Christian beliefs in a distinctive and persuasive way.

THE INTERPLAY OF CHARACTER AND CIRCUMSTANCE

Given that Douglass synthesized a belief system from various influences, the problem of how to write about his faith requires careful consideration. My approach to Douglass's moral and religious thought is indebted to the insights of several ethicists and theologians who examine literature utilizing the critical discipline of narrative analysis.

In the *Eclipse of Biblical Narrative*, Hans Frei calls attention to "the ongoing system of interactions," between characters and circumstances. Frei writes, "subject and social setting belong together, and characters and external circumstances fitly render each other."[10] Studies that prescind the subject from her setting fail to appreciate how these forces shape each other.

---

[10] Hans Frei, *The Eclipse of Biblical Narrative* (New Haven CT: Yale University Press, 1974) 13.

The dialectical relation between a subject and her social setting inspires a focus on narrative. By conjoining the insights of personal narrative, and the contributions of historical and philosophical analysis, one interrelates characters and circumstances. Descriptive accounts of this sort reflect not only mature characters but also the processes by which characters become mature. That is to say, one way to demonstrate how characters and external circumstances "fitly render each other" is to record how characters develop over time.

History establishes the temporal reality, and the external circumstances, within which the moral agent acts. Through the process of historical analysis, Douglass scholars can analyze the influential people and events that inspired Douglass's growth and that conspired to limit his growth. Events that appeared to Douglass as chance occurrences, as well as occurrences he failed to describe, exerted shaping influences on his thought. Historical analysis puts us in touch with these influences.

Narrative analysis is a helpful addition to historical and philosophical analysis in that it renders a "thick subject." In the case of autobiography, for example, the narrator's story discloses her perspective, her ideas, intentions, motivation, and fundamental orientation to her external reality. Story reveals that which its author wants us to know about herself and the things she considers to be important. Narrative analysis applied to the story may further disclose the tensions, contradictions and unfinished business that its author preferred we did not see.

This study first recommends an interpretive approach that begins with a commitment to the dialectical relation between Frederick Douglass and his social location. Starting with the premise that we are born into an ongoing story and that we are comprised of stories, the goal of maturation is to gain a comprehensive understanding of ourselves, to make sense of our stories. As we mature, we edit and reedit our stories along the time line and impositions of circumstance. We emphasize certain stories to the detriment of others, and we reconcile contentious roles (e.g., being black and American in the nineteenth century). In short, we define our truths and organize a discrete self. The process of maturation is replete with exaggeration, inconsistency, contradiction, tension, and unfinished business. The upshot is that the ideas expressed in Douglass's narratives, speeches, editorials, and other writings are best understood when illuminated by the integration of social-historical, philosophical, and narrative analysis.

Second, this interpretive account engages Douglass over a lengthy period of time. Unlike methodologies that treat mature thought exclusively, my account privileges developmental thought as well. It attempts to trace the ways in which Douglass's character was shaped by, and shaped, his circumstances.

Third, instead of making narrative fit its intellectual-historical period, the historical stage—the context into which the narrative is born—is set. Thus framed, the narrative itself discloses its intellectual-historical influences and milieu. The difference between this approach and others is more than semantic. Scholars run the risk of masking the characters they seek to render when they allow those characters to become markers for significant historical trends or events. Without appropriate narrative nuances, an appeal to the ebb and flow of the times can fail to explain those instances within the subject's moral and religious experience that flow counter to prevailing currents.

In depicting the circumstances and character of Frederick Douglass to illuminate his moral and religious thought from his early days in slavery to the end of the civil war, two features stand out:

(1) Douglass benefited from two sets of circumstances due to his particular origins. First, he benefited from a generalized set of socio-economic arrangements derived from the economy in Maryland during the first half of the nineteenth century. Second, he benefited from a more residual set of cultural and interpersonal arrangements due to his genealogical family, the community of slaves with whom he interacted, and the rapport enjoyed with his master's family.

(2) Douglass was a Christian. His commitment to the institution of the church waned over time, but he maintained an abiding belief in the bedrock Christian story. He also maintained

some degree of contact with either the AME or AME Zion Church for much of his life. The Christian story informed his understanding of his own life, his estimates of human good and evil, and his verdicts regarding slavery and equality. Christianity was an inheritance he received and interpreted, a faith system that shaped him and that he shaped.

SETTING THE STAGE

A narrative account of Frederick Douglass begins before his birth in 1818. In order to understand Douglass, one must first understand the environment into which he was born and those influences that shaped his early development. Douglass did not create himself *ex nihilo*. On the contrary, the circumstances of his birth and of his enslavement provide the content of his earliest lessons in life and set the parameters within which Douglass's character developed.

That Douglass was born a slave on the Eastern Shore of Maryland, in the nineteenth century, on a large plantation, has as much to do with the course of his life and his successes as does his character and agency. That he was raised within a community of Americanized slaves, several generations removed from Africa, and with an extended history on the Eastern Shore, are important to his early self-understanding and rapport with his master's family.

These circumstances, the external facts of Douglass's childhood, go relatively unnoticed in the body of Douglass's writings. Autobiographical narrative, the mainstay of Douglass's writings, privileges first-person agency. From that perspective, the social, economic, and political forces that shape communities and the ways in which they interact are downplayed. Further, Douglass wrote his first narrative to convince the public that he was indeed a fugitive slave. He made the case by providing first-hand accounts. The broader forces of his biography were outside his scope.

In order to locate Douglass within a social matrix, one must at the very least address five factors that shaped his social location.

These factors encompassing Douglass's socioeconomic setting, genealogy, and enslavement include: (1) historical period; (2) geography; (3) economic and political climate; (4) genealogy and family history; and, (5) interaction with individuals significant to his growth and development. In short, were it not for circumstance, for that confluence of social, historical, economic, demographic, and interpersonal forces that set his context and fed his character, it is likely that Frederick Douglass would have died anonymously in slavery.

HISTORICAL AND SOCIOLOGICAL BACKGROUND

Historians generally divide American slavery into two broad chronological periods, colonial (dating from 1619 to about 1770) and antebellum (dating from about 1800 to the Emancipation Proclamation of 1863). Colonial slavery was a system of labor designed to aid and abet European expansion into the British colonies of the New World. Before it became codified in the last decades of the seventeenth century and early eighteenth century, coerced labor was a condition among Europeans and Native Americans as well as among transplanted Africans. Though their numbers were small, some blacks owned the rights to other blacks and even to white indentured servants. Indeed, European indentured servants were the most numerous coerced laborers in the middle of the seventeenth century.

By the 1660s the picture changed. Several factors made slavery more attractive for those with means. The profitability of slavery vis-à-vis indentured servitude, predominant racial stereotypes about Africans, and British domination of the Atlantic precipitated the growth of the African slave trade. Concomitant with the expanding slave trade was the passage of slave codes. Virginia led the way and passed its first slave code in 1680. During the eighteenth century, the status of Africans relative to whites became codified and racial lines entrenched. Unlike the color-blind labor of the seventeenth century, eighteenth century slavery turned Africans into property. It deprived them of all vestiges of legal or social recourse, leaving them vulnerable to the whims of the dominant class. Not until the 1830s did abolitionists rally to their defense. From the time of Virginia's first slave code, the "peculiar institution," drew little public scrutiny for 150 years.

In addition to the legal and social sanctions accorded slavery, the eighteenth century is remarkable also for the exponential rise in American-born slaves. Unlike in South America, where the native slave population declined and slave imports had to be maintained, the native slave population in the colonies reproduced itself at a prolific rate. A fast rate of reproduction coupled with increased importation meant that in places like Virginia and South Carolina the proportion of blacks in the population grew by several hundred percent between 1680 and 1750.[11]

The Tidewater region of the Chesapeake colonies—Virginia, Maryland, and Northeastern North Carolina—experienced particularly rapid growth due to slavery. Historian Peter Kolchin states that "annual exports of tobacco (almost all from the Chesapeake colonies) surged from 20,000 pounds in 1619 to 38 million pounds in 1700."[12] Tobacco plantations in Virginia and Maryland, the most prosperous tobacco states, became the cornerstone of a rural Southern society and progenitor of a gentry class.

During the nineteenth century, however, tobacco fortunes began to decline in Maryland. As a result, Maryland became increasingly dissimilar to the other Southern slaveholding states in respect to its development of the "peculiar institution." Historian Barbara Fields portrays nineteenth century Maryland as under-going profound changes owing to the decline of tobacco fortunes and to the replacement of tobacco by cereal cultivation. As cereal cultivation replaced tobacco in Southern Maryland and on the Eastern Shore, the numbers of free blacks grew exponentially. Unlike the year-round labor demands of tobacco, cereal— primarily wheat—cultivation required only seasonal labor

---

[11] Peter Kolchin, *American Slavery: 1619–1877* (New York: Hill and Wang, 1993) 11.

[12] Ibid., 24.

demands. Slaveholders in the Southern colonies of Maryland and on the Eastern Shore, where Douglass was born, adapted to the new labor demands by routinely hiring out slaves.

Interestingly, Northern Maryland pursued industry and was not dependent upon slave labor to the extent of the other two regions in Maryland. Fields argues that between 1790 and 1850, the population data show "two Marylands evolving in different directions."[13] By 1850, Northern Maryland was an overwhelmingly white and free labor society. It was also home to almost 70 percent of the white population of Maryland.[14] Southern Maryland and the Eastern Shore, committed to agriculture and slavery, "grew increasingly isolated and stagnant."[15]

Relying extensively on the US Seventh Census (1850), Fields successfully demonstrates the extent of the changes that made Maryland unique among slaveholding states. In 1790, for example, slaves accounted for one-third of Maryland's population. By 1850, slaves accounted for less than one-sixth of Maryland's population.[16] Not only did the slave population decline in absolute numbers over the state as a whole, but moreover, they were the only segment of the population to do so.[17] The number of slaves in Maryland declined by approximately twelve percent between 1790 and 1850.[18] The figure is closer to nineteen percent when measured from 1810 to 1850.[19]

By way of comparison, the slave population in surrounding slaveholding regions grew prodigiously. In Virginia between 1790 and 1850, the slave population increased by sixty-one percent.[20] In North Carolina, it increased by 187 percent.[21] Slave populations in

---

[13] Barbara Fields, *Slavery and Freedom on the Middle Ground: Maryland During the Nineteenth Century* (New Haven CT: Yale University Press, 1985) 22.

[14] Ibid., 9.

[15] Ibid., 6–7.

[16] Ibid., 1.

[17] Ibid., 15.

[18] Ibid.

[19] Ibid.

[20] Ibid.

[21] Ibid.

South Carolina and Georgia grew by 259 percent and 1204 percent, respectively.[22]

If his birth in Maryland, as opposed to, say, Georgia, was a circumstantial blessing for Douglass, then so was his birth on the Eastern Shore. Whereas the slave population of Northern Maryland increased by five percent (a small figure in comparison to the 228 percent increase in the general population of Northern Maryland), and whereas the slave population of Southern Maryland declined by approximately two percent, the slave population of the Eastern Shore declined by nearly thirty-three percent between 1790 and 1850.[23] Fields concludes that "most of the loss to the slave population showed up as a gain to the free black population."[24] Accordingly, the proportion of free blacks in the total population of the Eastern Shore increased from approximately four percent to better than nineteen percent during the first half of the nineteenth century.[25]

These numbers reveal a good deal about the changes that were occurring within Maryland at the time of Douglass's birth. They demonstrate a sizeable and growing population of free blacks in that state and that, in Fields's words, "of the three regions, the Eastern Shore had the widest and most consistent experience of free black people and, consequently, of free black labor."[26]

Douglass knew of free blacks during his childhood years. This knowledge supported his belief that God did not intend for blacks to be slaves. The theory that God intended for blacks to be slaves and for whites to be slaveholders, a proposition slave children were taught as part of their religious indoctrination, did not satisfy Douglass: "I found that there were puzzling exceptions to this theory of slavery... I knew of blacks who were not slaves; I knew of whites who were not slaveholders; and I knew of persons who were nearly white, who were slaves. Color, therefore, was a

---

[22] Ibid.
[23] Ibid.
[24] Ibid.
[25] Ibid., 11.
[26] Ibid., 11–12.

very unsatisfactory basis for slavery."[27] The juxtaposition of slave and free blacks was an important part of Douglass's early experience.

This type of social juxtaposition was one of the special features of slavery in Maryland during the first half of the nineteenth century. It is one of four such features examined by Fields that made Maryland unique among slaveholding states. The other features include: the small size of slaveholdings; the heavy volume of slave trades; and the prominence of slave hiring.

Social Juxtaposition. Fields argues that interaction between slaves and free blacks in Maryland was commonplace. Given that Maryland had the largest free black population of any state,[28] and given the economic situation outlined above, it is not surprising that the worlds of slaves and free blacks became interconnected.[29]

Beyond the instances of joint labor, this interconnection often took the form of marriage. So common was the marriage of slaves and free blacks in Maryland, that Fields describes it as being "unremarkable."[30] Though unremarkable in frequency, marriage between slaves and free blacks is remarkable in that it often ended suddenly and unceremoniously when an enslaved spouse was sold. Black families were often torn apart by the sale of a family member. Douglass lamented this common practice as a "marked feature of the cruelty and barbarity of the slave system."[31]

Although there is no data to indicate the extent to which free blacks schooled slaves (in violation of slave statutes), their lives connected in this regard as well. According to Fields, the 1850 census estimates that better than fifty percent of the free black population in Maryland was at least minimally literate, or literate

---

[27] Frederick Douglass, *My Bondage and My Freedom* (New York, 1855), in Henry Louis Gates, Jr., ed. *Frederick Douglass/Autobiographies* (New York: Library of America/Penguin Books, 1994) 179.

[28] Fields, *Slavery and Freedom on the Middle Ground*, 29.

[29] Ibid., 28.

[30] Ibid.

[31] Douglass, *My Bondage and My Freedom*, 142.

to some degree.[32] It is likely that free blacks imparted their learning to slaves despite the legal and prevailing moral prohibitions against teaching slaves how to read.

The consequences of the juxtaposing interconnections were sometimes harmful but chiefly beneficial to the slaves. If a slave gained a new perspective about the possibilities of life beyond slavery, the slaveholder gained a new cause to exact harsh and vindictive penalties for infractions of prescribed duties. Nevertheless, to the slave, free blacks represented the hope of freedom. As Fields puts it, they "gave the lie to the prevailing racial justification for slavery, undermining the system's ideological underpinnings..."[33] To the slaveholder, free blacks represented the dissolution of the "peculiar institution." They were a threat to the prevailing customs and attitudes among slaves and slaveholders.

Free blacks demonstrated that, given autonomy, black people possessed the intelligence, diligence, and patience necessary to attain financial success and to interact with whites on equal terms. The example set by successful free blacks was incompatible with the continuing survival of slavery as an institution. Though they tried to control and limit the interaction of slave and free blacks, white farmers found that free blacks were an economic necessity. Social juxtaposition was an unavoidable consequence of the economic environment.

Small Size of Slaveholdings. Small slaveholdings were another of the contributing factors to the rise of a large, free black population in Maryland. Fields estimates that by 1860 only thirteen percent of white households in Maryland owned slaves.[34] Even in the counties of Southern Maryland and the Eastern Shore where slavery was more entrenched, fewer than one-third of white households held slaves.[35] Population data from the eighth US Census reveals that: "the most common slaveholding in Maryland by 1860 was one slave; half the slaveholders owned fewer than

---

[32] Fields, *Slavery and Freedom on the Middle Ground*, 39.
[33] Ibid., 39.
[34] Ibid., 227n35.
[35] Ibid.

three slaves, three-fourths fewer than eight, and 90 percent fewer than fifteen slaves."[36]

The upshot is twofold. First, the numbers substantiate the historical veracity of Douglass's testimony. Given the relative paucity of white slaveholding households, and the relatively large number of free blacks, it is not surprising that Douglass knew of whites who did not own slaves, and of blacks who were not slaves.

Second, the numbers disclose the special circumstance of slavery in Maryland. The median slave was likely to belong to an owner of two to three slaves.[37] Such slaveholdings were too small to accommodate entire black families, and were too small to generate profits during lean years.[38] Assuming that small planters were more vulnerable than large plantation owners to financial reverses, then small planters were more likely to liquidate their holdings.[39] That is to say, a depressed economy motivated small slaveholders to sell their slaves, to hire out their slaves, or to allow their slaves to purchase freedom. If fear of separation from family loomed heavily over slaves, then fear of financial ruin troubled Maryland's small slaveholders.[40] In order to offset financial ruin, the smaller slaveholders accommodated the social juxtaposition of slaves and free blacks.

Slave Trade Volume. The heavy volume of slave trading comprises a third index of Maryland's unique position among slave states. Trading took three forms: either interstate or intrastate sale, and interstate migration.[41] The most common of these was intrastate sale.[42] Fields estimates that roughly "12 percent of the total slave population of 1830 ended up on the [auction] block between then and 1840."[43] For the county of Douglass's birth, Talbot County, the figure was closer to 14 percent.[44] These

---

[36] Ibid., 24.
[37] Ibid., 25.
[38] Ibid., 24.
[39] Ibid., 26.
[40] Ibid.
[41] Ibid., 24.
[42] Ibid.
[43] Ibid.
[44] Ibid.

numbers underscore the high volume of slave trading in Maryland during the years of Douglass's childhood.

Prominence of Slave Hiring. In terms of frequency, trading was secondary only to slave hiring among Maryland slaveholders. Fields writes that "the small size of holdings" and the "variability of labor requirements" made hiring "much more common than sale."[45] By hiring out the services of a slave, a slaveholder could defer maintenance costs (that is to say, costs associated with feeding, sheltering, and clothing a slave) and accrue profit for the duration of the slave's contracted service.

The special circumstances of slavery in Maryland are confirmed in the Douglass narratives. During his twenty years as a slave, Douglass: (1) interacted with free blacks and eventually married a free black woman; (2) was the only slave of Hugh and Sophia Auld for a total of approximately ten years; (3) experienced intrastate migration a half-dozen times; (4) escaped the fate of roughly fifteen family members who were sold into Southern cotton states;[46] (5) was hired out by his master, Thomas Auld, for three years; (6) hired himself out for about three years before escaping to New York.

The autobiographical accounts of other Eastern Shore slaves bear out the distinctive features of slavery in Maryland during the first half of the nineteenth century. One must keep in mind, however, that published narratives tend to be written by slaves who were freed or who escaped from slavery. For this reason, they do not always provide particular names, places, and events with candor. In some instances these details were omitted to protect other slaves or to prevent recapture. Nevertheless, these narratives demonstrate that Douglass was not unlike other slaves in his judgments of freedom and slavery, or in his efforts at self-improvement. Four of these narratives will suffice to make the case.

Consider the story of William Green, whose narrative was published in 1853. Green was born on the Eastern Shore in Oxford

---

[45] Ibid., 27.
[46] Gates, *Autobiographies/Frederick Douglass*, 1051.

Neck. He describes his master, Edward Hamilton, as a "humane man" who was generally kind to his slaves "in the way of feeding and clothing them."[47] Green estimates that Hamilton owned eight or nine plantations. Like Douglass, Green made a decision to gain his freedom: "Having a great many relations who were almost all free, and I being a slave, made me very unhappy, and every day I became more and more determined to be free or die in the attempt."[48]

Green too recounts a fight with an overseer: "I jumps at him and snatches the whip from him; he aims another blow at me; I caught him by the collar and threw him upon the ground; and down upon the ground we had it; he and I, blow for blow, kick for kick, there we fought until almost out of breath. He cries out, 'let me be, let go of me.'"[49] After that experience, Green at times openly resisted his enslavement by refusing to perform prescribed duties. Eventually, he gained his freedom.

James Williams was also a slave on the Eastern Shore. He was born in Cecil County in 1825. His mother successfully escaped to Pennsylvania when he was a child. As a ten year old houseboy, Williams decided to run away as well. "Seeing the differences between freedom and slavery, I made up my mind that when I was old enough I would run away."[50] In 1838, the same year that Douglass escaped to New York, Williams took one of his master's horses and escaped in broad daylight. He made his way to Pennsylvania and found his mother.

The Reverend Noah Davis was born a slave in Madison County, Virginia, in 1804. Early religious training by his father led to a conversion experience, baptism, and ultimately to a position

---

[47] William Green, *Narrative of Events In the Life of William Green, Formerly a Slave* (Springfield MO: L. M. Guernsey, 1853) 4; James Weldon Johnson Collection, Yale University Library.

[48] Ibid., 5.

[49] Ibid., 12.

[50] James Williams, *Life and Adventures of James Williams, A Fugitive Slave, With a Full Description of the Underground Railroad* (San Francisco: Women's Union Print, 1873) 13; James Weldon Johnson Collection, Yale University Library.

as "missionary to the colored people of Baltimore."[51] Friends in Baltimore helped Davis to raise the five hundred dollars he needed to purchase his freedom. In 1847, Davis migrated from Virginia to Maryland. He found some differences between blacks in Baltimore and those he knew in Madison County: "When I was among the colored people of Baltimore, I found, to my surprise, that they were advanced in education, quite beyond what I had conceived of.... I had never had a day's schooling; and coming to one of the first cities in the union, where the colored people had the advantages of schools, and where their pulpits were occupied, Sabbath after Sabbath, by comparatively intelligent colored ministers—what could I expect..."[52] With considerable financial assistance, Davis eventually was able to purchase his wife and five of seven children. He published his story in the hope of raising enough money to purchase two sons who remained in slavery.

Finally, consider the story of Levi Jenkins Coppin, who was born on the Eastern Shore in 1848 and became a bishop in the African Methodist Episcopal Church. Unlike Green, Williams, and Davis, Coppin was born free. He writes that when he was about nine years old, his mother allowed him to work for a farmer named Perry Pennington. Coppin writes: "Pennington had no slaves of his own. One of the hired men that worked for him was a slave to another man, the rest were free people.... The wife of the slave man referred to was a free woman, and was Pennington's cook."[53]

The stories of Green, Williams, Davis, and Coppin contribute to our understanding of what life was like for blacks in Maryland during the first half of the nineteenth century. Their stories attest to the distinctiveness of slavery in Maryland. Each of the men interacted with free blacks, fugitive slaves, or blacks who hired out their services to white farmers and merchants. This interaction

---

[51] Noah Davis, *A Narrative of the Life of Reverend Noah Davis, A Colored Man* (Baltimore: John F. Weishampel, Jr., 1859) 10, 21, 35; James Weldon Johnson Collection, Yale University Library.

[52] Ibid., 35–36.

[53] L. J. Coppin, *Unwritten History* (New York: Negro Universities Press, repr.1968) 83–84; James Weldon Johnson Collection, Yale University Library.

contributed to their estimates of slavery and freedom, and to their determination to improve their lots in life. Slaves who escaped, like Williams, benefited from their proximity to Northern states. Free blacks who hired out their services, like Coppin, benefited from the socioeconomic conditions in Maryland that favored free labor.

These stories attest to more than merely the distinctive features of slavery in Maryland. James Williams, William Green, and Frederick Douglass, decided as children that they were going to be free. The socioeconomic climate that existed in Maryland is not sufficient to explain their decision. One must look also to interpersonal relationships.

GENEALOGICAL AND
INTERPERSONAL BACKGROUND

Beyond the influence of broader historical and socioeconomic currents, Douglass's character was also shaped by the families and individuals that populated his world as a child. Among the most significant people to Douglass were his family, the Baileys; his master's family, the Anthonys; and the family of his master's employer and plantation owner, the Lloyds.

Apart from the families mentioned, there were also many individuals who impressed Douglass with their kindness, vulnerability, humility, resolve, or cruelty. His narratives are compelling, in part, due to his detailed descriptions of the ways in which slaves, overseers, and masters interacted. In telling his story, Douglass provides the reader a tantalizing glimpse into the complex world of the slaves.

Douglass was born to a slave woman named Harriet Bailey and to a father who was believed to be white. Not much is known about Douglass's mother and even less about his father. Harriet Bailey was born on the Richard Skinner plantation in 1792. Five years later, Harriet and her mother, Betsy (or Betsey), were among several slaves transferred to Aaron Anthony when Anthony married Skinner's granddaughter. Douglass writes in 1855 that his mother was one of five girls born to Betsy Bailey. He lists his aunts as Jenny, Esther, Milly and Priscilla, but he omits his aunt Maryann, who was sold to an Alabama trader when Douglass was seven.[54] Interestingly, about a month or two before Maryann was traded, his Aunt Jennie and her husband, Noah, successfully escaped.

Douglass saw his mother only a handful of times. She was hired out as a field hand to a tenant farmer some ten to twelve miles from where her son lived. Occasionally, after working in the fields all day, she made the long journey to her son's quarters, staying just long enough to put him to sleep before returning to her own quarters.

The identity of Douglass's father remains a mystery. Given that Douglass had a much lighter complexion than either his mother or grandmother, and given the rumors that circulated among slaves at the time, Douglass's father was probably white. Some said that his master, Aaron Anthony, was his father. The Douglass narratives do not offer much pertinent speculation. In 1845, as a young abolitionist inveighing against the evils of slavery, Douglass wrote, "my father was a white man." Ten years later, as a famous orator and editor he wrote, "I say nothing of father because he was shrouded in a mystery." In his third autobiographical effort (1881), the aging statesman and lecturer wrote simply, "of my father, I know nothing." At times, Douglass speculated that plantation owner Edward Lloyd was his father, but there is little evidence to warrant that conclusion.

More is known about Douglass's maternal lineage. The Baileys hailed from a long established family of slaves in Talbot County. Harriet Bailey may have been able to read. Douglass credited his mother with his intellectual curiosity and ability. If anyone deserves credit for Douglass's curiosity, confidence, and acumen, it is probably his grandmother, Betsy Bailey. She was a remarkable woman of many talents. Douglass proclaimed that she was held in high esteem by both blacks and whites. Betsy Bailey made seine nets to sell; she worked as a midwife for pay; she grew

---

[54] Gates, *Autobiographies/Frederick Douglass*, 1050.

crops and fished as proficiently as any man; and, she cared for black children too young to perform the work of slaves. Douglass spent the first six years of his life under his grandmother's protective care.

Betsy Bailey's grandfather, Baly, is the earliest known member of the Bailey clan. Dickson Preston traced Baly to the Richard Skinner plantation in 1746. Skinner owned eleven slaves including Baly, who was approximately forty-five years old at the time.[55] According to Preston, from 1746 until Douglass's birth in 1818, neither Baly nor any of his descendants were sold away from the Eastern Shore.[56] On the contrary, they were "handed down from generation to generation, like family heirlooms."[57] That they were not sold and separated from one another over several generations suggests that Baly and his descendants may have developed cohesiveness as a family. Preston surmises that they did indeed develop a strong family bond:

> How strong this family loyalty was among the Baly-Baileys can be surmised from the one bit of tangible evidence: the persistence with which given names were passed on from mother to daughter, and even from unacknowledged father to son, through successive generations... Beginning with the original Baly, that name appears in five successive generations under various spellings (Baly, Bealy, Bail, Baley, Baily) until it finally emerged as Bailey, the family surname. Other given names also turned up with a regularity that could scarcely be coincidental... Even Augustus, Douglass's original second name, came to him from an uncle who had died shortly before the boy Frederick was born.[58]

---

[55] Dickson Preston, *Young Frederick Douglass: The Maryland Years* (Baltimore: Johns Hopkins University Press, 1980) 4.

[56] Ibid., 5.

[57] Ibid.

[58] Ibid., 5–6.

Preston's research into the Bailey clan provides additional evidence they possessed a sense of family heritage. It is likely, therefore, that the Bailey's roots in the colonial era and their relatively stable existence in the Eastern Shore had some positive impact on their ability to develop, maintain and transmit an enduring sense of family loyalty. Peter Kolchin's analysis lends credence to this view:

> The colonial era saw...the transformation of a society in which some people (relatively few, at first) were slaves into one in which slave labor formed the basis of the economy and social order. At first, novelty and experimentation characterized social relations: first- and second-generation slaves confronted first- and second-generation masters, most of whom were new not only to slavery but also to one another and indeed to America. Gradually, social patterns hardened: as masters and slaves were born into slave relations, behavior that had once been tentative and experimental became established and routine.[59]

Perhaps Baly experienced an opportunity, as social patterns hardened, to transmit the beliefs and values necessary for family loyalty to develop. Or perhaps Baly and his progeny were simply fortunate. Ultimately, whatever the reasons for their success, the Baileys were a strong and, in their own way, proud family, with deep roots in their Eastern Shore soil and a long tradition of courage and endurance. That makes it less surprising that they produced, out of the sordidness and poverty of slavery, the flowering genius of a Frederick Douglass.[60]

Preston is correct in maintaining that Douglass did indeed absorb a fundamental attitude or orientation from the Baileys.[61] Although it is difficult to dissect this orientation into specific

---

[59] Kolchin, *American Slavery*, 28–29.
[60] Preston, *Young Frederick Douglass*, 6.
[61] Ibid., 10.

beliefs, it is possible to see the ways in which Douglass benefited from the attitudes he gained from the Baileys. For example, the characteristic Bailey family attitude helps to explain Douglass's rapport with the Lloyd clan. Edward Lloyd was impressed with young Douglass not because of his differences from whites, but because of his similarities. Douglass was very inquisitive and quick to learn; he expressed himself clearly and effectively; and, generally, he was an engaging child. In recognition of his peculiarities, Edward Lloyd selected Douglass from among all the slave children on his plantation to become playmate to his son, Daniel. That Douglass displayed these unique character traits by age six is a tribute to his grandmother and the Bailey family heritage.

I do not maintain that Douglass was an exceptional child solely because of his family orientation. He had siblings who experienced, presumably, a similar orientation but without demonstrating Douglass's remarkable interpersonal skills. I suggest, rather, that the Bailey clan did transmit values to Douglass and that Douglass benefited from that heritage.

The influence of plantation owner Edward Lloyd was another circumstantial blessing in Douglass's life. Lloyd was not Douglass's owner, but by selecting Douglass to attend to his youngest son, Daniel, Lloyd rewarded Douglass's precociousness and retarded his development as either a field hand or a house servant. As Daniel's playmate, Douglass was spared the misery of the fields and the endless drudgery of the manor.

More significantly, Douglass was spared the realization of himself as either a field hand or a house servant. Slavery thrived by transforming blacks into personal property. By delaying Douglass's development into either a field hand or house servant, Lloyd impeded the process of dehumanization that could have made Douglass a pliant slave.

Douglass could self-consciously recognize that he was a slave, and even worse, a slave for life. The shock and horror of slavery were experiences noted by Douglass. But, as a youngster, he was not yet made to feel the daily routine and drudgery of slavery. On the contrary, as Daniel's playmate he was permitted the space necessary for exploration and contemplation. He was allowed to be "Freddy," when other slave children were learning to become chattel.

Lloyd's decision benefited Douglass in another way as well. Close and constant proximity to his twelve year old playmate exposed Douglass to what Preston aptly calls, "white habits of speech."[62] Douglass gained a distinctive style or mode of discourse from the Lloyds, one that must have sounded peculiar coming from a slave boy, yet endeared him to his captors.

His friendship with Daniel Lloyd also taught Douglass a lesson or two about power and protection. Douglass considered Daniel to be a friend; one of only two friends acknowledged during his early years. Daniel answered many of Douglass's questions. Occasionally he gave Douglass a piece of cake, or some such item, as a token of friendship. Daniel also protected Douglass from bigger boys who derided the young slave's peculiar bearing and speech.

Daniel Lloyd was not the only white person to protect Douglass. When he was not up at the great house with Daniel, Douglass also received special consideration at home. His master, Aaron Anthony, and Anthony's twenty year old daughter, Lucretia Auld, treated Douglass more like a child than a slave. Douglass admits, somewhat grudgingly, that the "little attention" he received from his master was "remarkably mild and gentle."[63] Douglass wrote: "Capt. Anthony could be kind, and, at times, he even showed an affectionate disposition. Could the reader have seen him gently leading me by the hand—as he sometimes did—patting me on the head, speaking to me in soft, caressing tones and calling me his 'little Indian boy,' he would have deemed him a kind old man, and, really, almost fatherly."[64] This description counters Douglass's depiction of his master as being "insensible to the claims of humanity."[65] No doubt Anthony was

---

[62] Ibid., 55.
[63] Douglass, *My Bondage and My Freedom*, 171.
[64] Ibid., 172.
[65] Ibid., 171.

capable of cruelty, but his general behavior toward Douglass was moderate.

Anthony's daughter, Lucretia Auld, also made Douglass feel special. He cites her as his other friend. Whereas Daniel Lloyd protected Douglass and taught him "many things," Lucretia Auld favored Douglass with pity. When Douglass sang under her window, she rewarded his efforts with bread and butter. When Douglass was bruised in an altercation with slave boys from the Lloyd farm, Lucretia dressed his wounds and healed his spirit. In sum, both the Lloyds and the Anthonys took an unusual interest in Douglass. That interest was a boon to his development.

The major events of Douglass's life as a slave correspond to the patterns and peculiarities of slavery in Maryland. Insofar as these events informed his character, there is a compelling relationship to be discerned between that character and the pattern of slavery, the circumstances into which he was born.[66]

---

[66] I do not suggest that circumstance exhaustively determines character. My claim is more modest. One's character cannot be properly assessed apart from a consideration of the circumstances prior to and during the formation of that character. My point is character alone does not adequately explain Douglass's successes. It does not account for the intricacies of his moral thought. Douglass's thinking reflected his experience as a slave. His was a unique experience. He was a slave, but he was a privileged slave. He was exposed to the same vulnerability, helplessness, and dread that other black slaves faced, but he also experienced protection, friendship, and care from several white slave owners.

2

THE SLAVE EPISODE

Reflecting on his early days in slavery, Douglass commented, "A man's character greatly takes its hue and shape from the form and color of things about him."[1] Indeed, the hue and shape of Douglass's childhood was vital to what Benjamin Quarles calls the "savor" of his personality.[2] Quarles is skeptical that the rigorous historian can confidently say Douglass's case against slavery was based "exclusively" on his experiences.[3] Nevertheless, Quarles concedes Douglass's memories must have played some part in his polemic.[4] The questions at hand are: (1) What did Douglass remember about his experiences in slavery; and, (2) How significant were those memories to his case against slavery?

The experiences of twenty years in slavery Douglass recorded in his autobiographical accounts can be grouped by any number of themes or categories. I favor six: (1) maternal influences; (2) introduction to slavery; (3) the Baltimore experience; (4) early moral and religious lessons; (5) the Covey experience;

---

[1] Frederick Douglass, *My Bondage and My Freedom* (New York, 1855), in Henry Louis Gates, Jr., ed. *Frederick Douglass/Autobiographies* (New York: Library of America/Penguin Books, 1994) 171.
[2] Benjamin Quarles, *Frederick Douglass* (New York: Atheneum, 1968) 8.
[3] Ibid.
[4] Ibid.

and, (6) escape attempts. These themes are not intended to collect every experience that Douglass recalled, but rather to sort out the experiences he believed vital to his development. I begin with Douglass's earliest recollections about slavery.

MATERNAL INFLUENCES

Douglass scarcely mentioned his grandmother in his first autobiography, *Narrative of the Life of Frederick Douglass*. His aim was to convince a skeptical public that he had been a slave. He certainly did not have the appearance or manner of a fugitive slave when he came into public prominence in 1841. He did not speak like a slave or carry himself like a slave. Proponents of slavery were quick to accuse him of fabricating the events of which he spoke. To counter allegations of impropriety, Douglass put to paper a record of his experiences in slavery. The record was so explicit and detailed that it quelled any question of its veracity. In accordance with his aim, Douglass included only that information he believed essential to establishing his case against slavery. He refrained from what he deemed to be extraneous detail, information about his life that did not bear directly on his existence as a slave.

In 1893, the year that he published the final version of his autobiography, *Life and Times of Frederick Douglass*, Douglass had a much different reason for writing. There was no skeptical public to win over, no pro-slavery arguments to defeat. His purpose in writing was to establish his legacy, and by so doing, to locate his life and its significance in formative personal and national events. Relying on his earlier narratives for the explicit details that a seventy-four year old mind is apt to forget, Douglass offered a masterful commentary on his life and on the age in which he lived.

Due to his purposes in writing an 1845 autobiographical narrative, Douglass had neglected including information about his grandmother. It had not seemed pertinent in those earlier years. Yet the information in fact affords invaluable insight into his early formation. In an 1855 narrative, and later in the 1893 narrative, he devoted several pages to his earliest recollections of life with his grandmother. It is here that we catch our first glimpse of Douglass's moral development. What strikes us initially is that he learned many other things before he knew himself to be a slave,[5] and that was fundamental to the tone and tenor of his life.

Douglass minced no words about the significance of his grandmother to his earliest years. He wrote simply, "my grand-mother was all the world to me."[6] During those first years of childhood, before he was old enough to work in the fields, Douglass experienced caring love. He played with the other young children under his grandmother's watch, he explored the plantation with an abandon unknown to older slaves, and his eyes were opened to the wonders of nature.

Although the early days were filled with wonder and joy, Douglass also began to experience an anxiety that encroached on the relatively carefree nature of his childhood. This anxiety resulted from the knowledge that all he could see, every tree he climbed, every cabin he entered, the old well from which he could draw water without assistance, everything belonged to "a myster-ious personage" called "old master."[7] He learned the "sad fact" that his grandmother did not own her house, the house of his childhood, for this too belonged to the master. He learned the "sadder fact" that even his grandmother herself and all the children she cared for belonged to the master. Finally, he learned that he too belonged to Captain Aaron Anthony: "I learned this old master, whose name seemed ever to be mentioned with fear and shuddering, only allowed the little children to live with grandmother for a limited time, and that as soon as they were big enough they were promptly taken away to live with the said old

---

[5] Douglass, *Life and Times,* 478. In his final autobiography, Douglass wrote: "Living thus with my grandmother, whose kindness and love stood in place of my mother's, it was some time before I knew myself to be a slave. I knew many other things before I knew that."

6. Douglass, *Life and Times,* 479.

[7] Ibid.

master. These were distressing revelations, indeed."[8] The reckless abandon of youth was tempered by fear and dread; fear of his master and dread of the inevitable separation from his grandmother. For Douglass, slavery was a learned condition that stood in stark contrast to the freedom and care he experienced with his grandmother.

All in all, however, the distress of being a young slave did not outweigh its pleasures. Douglass recalled that he was "never expected to act like a little gentleman."[9] "Freed from all restraint, the slave-boy can be a genuine boy, doing whatever his boyish nature suggests."[10] Douglass availed himself of the privilege, and dealt with the accompanying distress as "water on a duck's back."[11]

That his earliest years were positive ones, filled as they were with wonder and joy has, again, formative significance. It is as a result of those early relationships with his mother and grand-mother that Douglass learned his first lessons about himself. In later years, he recalled his grandmother as "a woman of power and spirit," and "remarkably straight in figure, elastic and muscular in movement."[12]

In addition to the love and affection he experienced from his grandmother, there is one incident involving his mother that is of profound moral consequence. The setting is shortly after he was removed from his grandmother. He recalled being entrusted to the care of Aunt Katy and Aunt Esther. Aunt Katy was particularly cruel in her treatment of Douglass. He was beaten and starved as punishment while under her care. During one such attempt to punish him by making him go hungry, his mother came to his defense. After working all day in the fields she walked twelve miles from her own plantation to visit her son. When she learned of Aunt Katy's treatment of Douglass, she fed her son and scolded Katy in his presence. The influence of his mother's words may

---

[8] Ibid.
[9] Douglass, *My Bondage and My Freedom*, 144.
[10] Ibid.
[11] Ibid., 145.
[12] Douglass, *Life and Times*, 480.

have been of short duration on Katy, but they were of lasting duration on Douglass.

> I shall never forget the indescribable expression of her countenance when I told her that Aunt Katy had said she would starve the life out of me. There was deep and tender pity in her glance at me, and at the same moment, a fiery indignation at Aunt Katy...That night I learned as I had never learned before, that I was not only a child, but somebody's child. I was grander upon my mother's knee than a king upon his throne...I do not remember ever seeing her again.[13]

Before he knew that he was a slave, Frederick Douglass knew that he was somebody's child. His sense of being was grounded in maternal love. This final remembered meeting with his mother emphatically confirmed that knowledge. Douglass was aware of himself as being significant before he became another's chattel.

He was aware as well of the dignity and strength of his mother and grandmother. They not only promoted Douglass's growing sense of self, but were also heroic, if tragic, role models. As heroic figures they stood against the institution of slavery. As vulnerable individuals they ultimately succumbed to its intractable might. Beyond their influence on his character, Douglass's moral thought was shaped by interactions with his mother and grandmother. For example, years later Douglass indicated that the memory of his grandmother entered into his fulmination against slavery: "If any one thing in my experience, more than another, served to deepen my conviction of the infernal character of slavery, and to fill me with unutterable loathing of slaveholders, it was their base ingratitude to my poor old grandmother."[14]

---

[13] Ibid., 483–84.

[14] Frederick Douglass, *Narrative of the Life of Frederick Douglass, An American Slave, Written by Himself* (Boston: 1845), in Henry Louis Gates, Jr., ed. *Frederick Douglass/Autobiographies* (New York: Library of America/Penguin Books, 1994) 47. When these memoirs were first published, Douglass believed that the woman who provided him harbor against the cruelty

As for his mother, he attributed to her his zeal for knowledge though he only saw her four or five times in his life.

> I have since learned that she was the only one of all the colored people of Tuckahoe who could read. How she acquired this knowledge I know not, for Tuckahoe was the last place in the world where she would have been likely to find facilities for learning. I can therefore fondly and proudly ascribe to her an earnest love of knowledge. That in any slave state a field-hand should learn to read is remarkable, but the achievement of my mother, considering the place and circumstances, was very extraordinary.[15]

Douglass believed the woman who swept him up in her "strong protecting arms," and who died in "weariness and heartfelt sorrow" a few years later, was the source of that which made him his own master—an earnest love of knowledge.[16]

---

of slavery with power and spirit had been turned out to die in her elder years. He learned many years that was not the case. Yet, the supposition that his grandmother had been victimized by such inhumane treatment served to strengthen his indictment of slavery as an evil system.

[15] Douglass, *Life and Times,* 484.

[16] The maternal influence on Douglass constitutes a first narrative strand. Each successive strand, each experience, each memory, is grafted onto this one. If the maternal influence on Douglass was not a first narrative strand, then the shock and horror of slavery might have overwhelmed the seven-year-old boy, in effect crippling his moral development. That he had the wherewithal to learn to read and write suggests that the shock of slavery did not accomplish its task; it failed to negate the positive impact of the care and protection received in his first years. Though he occupied the role of slave, he was given the requisite moral space by blacks and whites alike to deny that the role of slave was appropriate to his true character. His fervent drive to be free was fueled by a deep-seated conviction that he was meant to be free; that somehow freedom was more constitutive of his character than was slavery. He never acquiesced to servitude. Before he knew what it meant to be a slave, he knew that he was an authentic "somebody," and that knowledge made him unfit to be a slave.

INTRODUCTION TO SLAVERY

Young Frederick was introduced into slavery as were other slave children, by abandonment. One day he was safe in his grandmother's caring love and the next he was delivered to his master's plantation some twelve miles away. Told to play with siblings Perry, Sarah and Eliza to whom he was just introduced, Douglass feared that his grandmother might leave him behind. She looked sad and was not behaving as usual. Douglass's fears proved to be well-founded. He wrote of the episode:

> ...one of the children, who had been in the kitchen, ran up to me, in a sort of roguish glee, exclaiming, "Fed, Fed! grandmammy gone! grandmammy gone!" I could not believe it; yet, fearing the worst, I ran into the kitchen, to see for myself, and found it even so. Grandmammy had indeed gone, and was now far away...I fell upon the ground, and wept a boy's bitter tears, refusing to be comforted....I had never been deceived before; and I felt not only grieved at parting...but indignant that a trick had been played upon me in a matter so serious. [17]

Deception and abandonment were the first realities of slavery for Douglass; grief, fear, and indignation his earliest response.

Apart from his recollections of grief and indignation, Douglass also drew on his memories to argue the immorality of slavery as an institution. "There is not, beneath the sky, an enemy to filial affection so destructive as slavery. It had made my brothers and sisters strangers to me; it converted the mother that bore me, into a myth; it shrouded my father in mystery, and left me without an intelligible beginning in the world."[18]

His introduction to slavery encompassed much more than just the grief, fear, and indignation felt when his grandmother abandoned him. Whippings were the most obvious and prevalent

---

[17] Douglass, *My Bondage and My Freedom*, 150.
[18] Ibid., 157.

feature of slavery. The whip was the first terror of slavery. A cursory glance at slave narratives provides numerous references to accounts of savage beatings. The practice was so extensive that good overseers were often distinguished from bad in that they did not seem to take as much pleasure in the whippings.[19]

Because they were more than merely punitive measures, whippings instilled fear and obedience in slaves. In his autobiography, titled *Twelve Years A Slave*, Solomon Northup attested: "Then the fears and labors of another day begin; and until its close there is no such thing as rest. He fears he will be caught lagging through the day; he fears to approach the gin-house with his basket-load of cotton at night; he fears when he lies down that he will oversleep himself in the morning."[20] The constant fear of whippings held the vast majority of slaves in check and in a constant state of anxiety. Former slave Austin Steward wrote, "It is this continual dread of some perilous future that holds in check every joyous emotion, every lofty aspiration, of the most favored slave..."[21]

At least three observations can be made about whippings and their impact. First, they were commonplace: "The whip is all in all. It is supposed to secure obedience to the slaveholder, and is held as a sovereign remedy among the slaves themselves, for every form of disobedience, temporal or spiritual. Slaves as well as slaveholders use it with an unsparing hand."[22] Second, whippings were acts of negative reinforcement, used to squelch any desire for freedom smoldering in the slave. Finally, they proved effective. Whippings were a primary means by which the shock of slavery was continually renewed in the life of the slave.

---

[19] Frederick Douglass, *Narrative of the Life of Frederick Douglass*, 22.

[20] Solomon Northup, *Twelve Years A Slave. Narrative of Solomon Northup, A Citizen of New York, Kidnaped in Washington City in 1841, and Rescued in 1853, From a Cotton Plantation Near the Red River, in Louisiana* (Auburn NY: Derby and Miller, 1853) in Willie Lee Rose, ed. *A Documentary History of Slavery in North America* (New York: Oxford University Press, 1976) 311.

[21] Austin Steward, *22 Years A Slave and 40 Years A Freeman* (Massachusetts: Addison-Wesley Company, repr. 1969), 22–23.

[22] Douglass, *My Bondage and My Freedom*, 165–66.

Douglass was no exception. His first reflection on what it meant to be a slave involved the vicious whipping of a woman who cared for him, Aunt Esther. More than the circumstances surrounding the whipping, it is Douglass's response that concerns us. He wrote in his 1845 narrative: "I was so terrified and horror-stricken at the sight, that I hid myself in a closet, and dared not venture out till long after the bloody transaction was over. I expected it would be my turn next. It was all new to me. I had never seen any thing like it before."[23]

The public spectacle accomplished its aim. Esther was punished for an infraction of her master's edicts. The horror of the spectacle demonstrated the master's absolute power over the slaves and his willingness to apply the lash if his will was not followed to the letter. The whipping of Esther filled Douglass with looming fear, or what Steward has aptly called "the dread of some perilous future." He believed that he would soon receive similar punishment for some unforeseen infraction.

This anxious and fearful anticipation of the lash accounted for at least two developments in Douglass's maturation. First, it introduced Douglass to the slave's life.[24] Second, as he witnessed the whipping of Esther in particular, and of other slaves in general, he came to identify intimately with the slaves' plight. Not long after his full immersion into slavery, Douglass began to taste its "soul-killing effects."[25]

By the age of seven, Douglass, who had thought of himself as a significant self learned that he was inconsequential under the law of the slaveholding South. Slavery took his family away from him, it sought to vanquish utterly his early perceptions of significance and self. It did not, however, completely extinguish his sense of personal dignity or the difficult hope of liberation. Douglass wrote later, somewhat triumphantly, "Young as I was I was already a fugitive from slavery in spirit and purpose."[26]

---

[23] Douglass, *Narrative of the Life of Frederick Douglass*, 19. Douglass refers to her as Aunt Hester to protect her identity.

[24] Ibid., 34.

[25] Ibid., 24.

[26] Douglass, *Life and Times*, 499.

If we think of Douglass's introduction to slavery in light of the maternal care he experienced, then we can see how Douglass began to order two contradictory indices of self-worth. He learned a few of the lessons of slavery, but those lessons did not negate the lessons of an earlier school.

Just seven years old, Frederick Douglass had arrived at a precarious juncture. The dread of a perilous future contradicted his positive appraisal of self-worth. Yet, the dominant spirit of his maternal influences helped him to make sense of himself. This spirit continued to benefit him through the care he received from two white women, Lucretia Auld, and her sister-in-law, Sophia Auld. What emerged was a slave, but a slave who nevertheless possessed a strong sense of self, a desire to be free, and who was coming to view himself included within God's providence. "From my earliest recollection, I date the entertainment of a deep conviction that slavery would not always be able to hold me within its foul embrace; and in the darkest hours of my career in slavery, this living word of faith and spirit of hope departed not from me, but remained like ministering angels to cheer me through the gloom. This good spirit was from God, and to him I offer thanksgiving and praise."[27]

As will be seen, Douglass had good reason to give thanks.

BALTIMORE

Douglass was not quite ten years old when he was taken from Eastern Shore, Maryland, and sent to Baltimore to live with Hugh and Sophia Auld. The importance of the move for his development cannot be overestimated. He wrote, "I may say here, that I regard my removal from Col. Lloyd's plantation as one of the most interesting and fortunate events of my life."[28] The move filled Douglass with hope. He had heard of Baltimore and longed to see the big city for himself.

---

[27] Douglass, *Narrative of the Life of Frederick Douglass*, 36.
[28] Douglass, *My Bondage and My Freedom*, 212.

As it turned out, the Baltimore experience was critical to Douglass's emerging character and thought. He learned to read in Baltimore, and in reading the noble ideals of abolitionists in light of his experience, he gained a more comprehensive grasp of the case for freedom.

The implications of such an important development were not lost on Douglass:

> ...it is quite probable that, but for the mere circumstance of being thus removed before the rigors of slavery had fastened upon me; before my young spirit had been crushed under the iron control of the slave-driver, instead of being, today, a FREEMAN, I might have been wearing the galling chains of slavery. I have sometimes felt, however, that there was something more intelligent than chance, and something more certain than luck, to be seen in the circumstance. If I have... worthily discharged the duties of a member of an oppressed people; this little circumstance must be allowed its due weight in giving my life that direction... I may be deemed superstitious and egotistical, in regarding this event as a special inter-position of Divine Providence in my favor; but the thought is a part of my history...[29]

Though Douglass's spirit was healthy, it took Baltimore to consolidate his passion for freedom. So necessary was the circumstance, so essential to his life's vocation, that Douglass was hard pressed in later years to see the relocation as merely chance or luck. From the vantage point of hindsight, with the faith of a believer, Douglass perceived God's hand in his deliverance from Tuckahoe. The event became part of his master story; it shaped the way in which he understood his world; it strengthened his core conviction of a just God, and it undergirded the basic assumptions

---

[29] Ibid., 212–13.

and expectations that propelled his actions.[30] Living in Baltimore became a pivotal point in his story. Without Baltimore, Douglass might have become just another slave.

Apart from the aura and the clamor of the big city, Douglass was impressed by the gentleness and kindness of his new mistress, Sophia Auld. Douglass took pains in his later narratives to record her "natural goodness of heart" and "benignant countenance." He came to regard her "as something more akin to a mother than a slaveholding mistress."[31] Douglass was entrusted to Sophia's exclusive management during his first year or two in Baltimore. He later wrote: "In hands so tender as hers, and in the absence of the cruelties of the plantation, I became, both physically and mentally, much more sensitive to good and ill treatment."[32] Auld treated Douglass more like a child than an object of possession. He, in turn, became sensitized to her care and responded to her as any child might to a loving adult, and not as a slave to his mistress. He asked her to teach him how to read, his desire roused by her reading of Scripture. She consented to his request and began by teaching Douglass the alphabet and small words.

Sophia's kindness was only one of the benefits of living with the Aulds in Baltimore. His accommodations were more to his liking. Carpets and straw beds replaced the cold, damp floor of his old master's kitchen; clean clothes replaced the tow-linen shirt he used to wear; bread and occasionally mush replaced the coarse cornmeal that he formerly ate for breakfast. Further, his work consisted only of running errands and taking care of the Auld's young son, Tommy. Douglass summed-up his first years in Baltimore, "I was really well off."[33]

The joy of those early years in Baltimore, however, was short-lived. Upon learning that his wife was teaching Frederick how to read, Mr. Auld promptly ended the lessons with an impassioned and prophetic speech. He explained, within earshot of

---

[30] Michael Goldberg, quoted in Peter Steinfels, "Beliefs," *New York Times*, 15 March 1995.

[31] Douglass, *My Bondage and My Freedom*, 215.

[32] Ibid., 216.

[33] Ibid.

Douglass, the dangers of teaching a slave to read; "it would forever unfit him for the duties of a slave."[34] Douglass wrote of Master Hugh's exposition:

> The effect of his words, *on me*, was neither slight nor transitory. His iron sentences—cold and harsh—sunk deep into my heart, and stirred up not only my feelings into a sort of rebellion, but awakened within me a slumbering train of vital thought..."Very well," thought I; "knowledge unfits a child to be a slave." I instinctively assented to the proposition; and from that moment I understood the direct pathway from slavery to freedom.[35]

Douglass was about twelve years old when he took this critical step toward freedom. He became resolute in seeking education, and continued his reading and spelling lessons with the assistance of local white youth. Douglass carried a copy of Webster's spelling book and "tuition" with which to pay his young teachers. "I generally paid my tuition fee to the boys, with bread, which I also carried in my pocket. For a single biscuit, any of my hungry little comrades would give me a lesson more valuable to me than bread."[36] The lessons began to reap rewards within a year, and Douglass was soon able to read such tracts as *The Columbian Orator*. For the first time, he was exposed to arguments for emancipation based on the claims of eternal justice and the innate rights of man. The speeches bolstered Douglass's faith: "If I ever wavered under the consideration, that the Almighty, in some way, ordained slavery, and willed my enslavement for his own glory, I wavered no longer. I had now penetrated the secret of all slavery and oppression, and had ascertained their true foundation to be in the pride, the power, and the avarice of man."[37]

Learning to read opened his mind to knowledge and, subsequently, to moral reflection. Knowledge opened his eyes to

---

[34] Ibid., 217.
[35] Ibid., 217-18.
[36] Ibid., 224.
[37] Ibid., 226.

the truth of his condition and awakened in him a loathing of all slaveholders, even benign ones. Knowledge also opened his eyes to slavery as an institution and enabled Douglass to transcend his own particular condition. He felt cheated; deliberately held in ignorance, and as a result saw slaveholders as a band of accomplished liars and robbers.[38] Learning to read enabled Douglass to bring a universal perspective to his estimation of slavery. As an institution, slavery was in part successful because it disallowed the slave the space necessary for moral reflection and kept her focused on the whip. Douglass, however, could now see his plight as part of the plight of all slaves. He understood that even mild treatment from masters was nevertheless abuse from slaveholders' hands.

Consider an excerpt from *The Columbian Orator* to which Douglass made reference. The piece is a dialogue between a master and slave that illuminates Douglass's universal perspective in the estimation of slavery:

> Master. It is in the order of providence that one man should become subservient to another. It ever has been so, and ever will be. I found the custom and did not make it.
>
> Slave. You cannot but be sensible, that the robber who puts a pistol to your breast may make just the same plea. Providence gives him a power over your life and property; it gave my enemies a power over my liberty. But it has also given me legs to escape with; and what should prevent me from using them? Nay, what should restrain me from retaliating the wrongs I have suffered, if a favorable occasion should offer?
>
> Master. Gratitude! I repeat, gratitude! Have I not endeavored ever since I possessed you to alleviate your misfortunes by kind treatment; and does that confer no obligation? Consider how much worse your condition might have been under another master.

---

[38] Ibid., 228.

Slave. You have done nothing for me more than for your working cattle. Are they not well fed and tended? Do you work them harder than your slaves? Is not the rule of treating both designed only for your own advantage?[39]

Reading *The Columbian Orator* helped Douglass to express why he was discontented with the relatively mild nature of his enslavement in Baltimore. Adequate clothing, shelter, and food could not offset the value of the liberty that slavery kept from him. Douglass was no longer the "light-hearted, gleesome boy" who came to live with the Aulds.[40] He became a tormented individual, gloomy and miserable, perceiving no way of escaping his bonds. The idea that he was a slave for life was to Douglass's mind more lamentable than the conditions of his servitude. Without the means to claim his God-given liberty, he was truly enslaved.

Sophia Auld reacted to Douglass's new demeanor with uncharacteristic harshness. Perhaps she believed him ungrateful. His discontented, downcast look soon grew offensive to her. Douglass interpreted the significance of this change in her demeanor as an indication of the irreducible difference between slave and master. "Nature had made us friends; slavery made us enemies."[41] His eyes opened to the truth of slavery, Douglass could see how Sophia's personality was warped under the weight of the "peculiar institution." Not only did he loathe slaveholders, he also pitied those who were unable to perceive the deleterious effects of slavery on their own spirits. He wrote, "we were both victims to the same overshadowing evil—she, as mistress, I, as slave."[42]

The advance against his enslavement that Douglass was able to make in Baltimore owed much to circumstance, to his own resolve and to the relatively kind treatment received from the Aulds. That kind treatment was especially important. Without it,

[39] Val J. Halamandaris, *The Columbian Orator* (Washington DC: Caring Publications, repr. 1997) 187.
[40] Douglass, *My Bondage and My Freedom*, 227.
[41] Ibid., 228.
[42] Ibid.

Douglass would not have enjoyed the time necessary for reading lessons and for moral reflection. His words are best:

> Beat and cuff your slave, keep him hungry and spiritless and he will follow the chain of his master like a dog; but feed and clothe him well, work him moderately, surround him with physical comfort, and dreams of freedom intrude. Give him a bad master, and he aspires to a good master; give him a good master and he wishes to become his own master. Such is human nature. You may hurl a man so low beneath the level of his kind, that he loses all just ideas of his natural position, but elevate him a little, and the clear conception of rights rises to life and power, and leads him onward.[43]

Douglass referred to his experience to reveal the immoral logic of slavery and to explain why his situation in Baltimore was a blessing. He was in jeopardy of losing his "natural position" when on the plantation. Baltimore afforded him "a good master" and greater physical comfort, with the result that he desired to become his own master. The circumstance of living in Baltimore shaped not only the form of his moral judgments, but also their content. The form became decidedly universal, the content emphatically abolitionist.

EARLY RELIGIOUS LESSONS

> Why am I a slave? Why are some people slaves, and others masters? Was there ever a time when this was not so? How did the relation commence?[44]

These sorts of questions figure among the earliest ones Douglass entertained about his slave status while a young boy on the Lloyd

---

[43] Ibid., 297.
[44] Ibid., 178.

plantation. The questions came about as a result of the brutal floggings of his Aunt Esther and of a cousin from Tuckahoe. Witnessing some of the "gross features" of slavery prompted Douglass to attempts at self-examination.[45] His attempts led him to questions about the character of God. Douglass, along with the other children, was sent to Isaac Copper—Uncle Isaac—to learn the Lord's Prayer.[46] Douglass did not discuss the efficacy of his encounter with Uncle Isaac. Rather, he reflected on his inquiries to the other children about God: "I learned from these inquiries, that "God, up in the sky," made everybody; and that he made white people to be masters and mistresses, and black people to be slaves. This did not satisfy me, nor lessen my interest in the subject."[47]

Far from lessening his interest, the responses elicited from other children only slightly older than Douglass introduced a paradox begging resolution. He was told that God was good but this answer did not help to explain the cruel treatment Aunt Esther endured. Douglass instinctively drew a large distinction between notions of goodness and Esther's punishment. "It was not good to let old master cut the flesh off Esther, and make her cry so."[48] At the time, Douglass concluded that God may have made white men to be slaveholders, but He did not make them to be bad slaveholders. Douglass thought bad slaveholders would surely be punished for their iniquities. His notions of God and of goodness did not fit with the cruelties of slavery. Douglass continued to question the relation between God and the "peculiar institution." He wrote in his 1855 narrative: "I was not very long in finding out the true solution of the matter. It was not color, but crime, not God, but man, that afforded the true explanation of the existence of slavery; nor was I long in finding out another important truth, viz: what man can make, man can unmake."[49]

The exact source of these conclusions is unclear. In this context the excerpt establishes the point at which Douglass came

---

[45] Ibid., 179.
[46] Ibid., 165.
[47] Ibid., 178.
[48] Ibid.
[49] Ibid., 179.

to an understanding of slavery as an evil perpetuated by whites, and not as a good ordained by God.

This view of slavery did not develop in a vacuum. Douglass's reasoning shows signs of what Riggins R. Earl, Jr., has called an "unofficial answer" to the morality of slavery shared in secret among slaves.[50] Douglass clearly endorsed a perspective that countered the approbation and "official answer" of slaveholders. Douglass's interaction with fellow slaves on the Eastern Shore helped him to appraise the morality of slavery. Given his social location, what he saw of slavery, and what he knew of freedom, Douglass was persuaded at an early age that slavery was a criminal institution of oppression.

Several points are significant here: (1) Douglass thought of slavery as a matter of moral and religious concern while still a child; (2) he understood that two answers to the morality of slavery were available to him; and, (3) he took a significant step toward becoming a mature moral agent by embracing one of those alternatives. His decision was, in part, based on an appeal to personal experience and trust in the testimony of slaves.

Douglass's next step forward in mature religious thinking occurred in Baltimore when he was approximately thirteen years old. By this time he was able to read and had garnered all the information he could on abolition and the abolitionists. His persistent efforts to learn to read and write was in defiance of Master Hugh Auld's contrary and explicit directive. Having already decided that slavery was criminal, Douglass developed an elaborate and creative scheme to continue learning. He enticed young, white schoolboys to aid him, unbeknownst to them.

Douglass learned from his master that education was a means of resistance to slavery, but he was less certain about religion's role in that regard. He believed that slavery was not of divine origin. God remained obscure to Douglass, hidden in platitudes

---

[50] Riggins R. Earl, Jr., "The Genesis of Douglass' Moral Understanding While A Slave: A Methodological Approach to Freedom," *The Journal of the Interdenominational Theological Center*, 9 (Fall, 1981): 19–29.

and prayers. While in Baltimore, Douglass had his first experience of a personal encounter with God.

Beyond formal religious doctrine, Douglass came to need God, "as a father and protector."[51] This longing for God was intensified by the preaching of a white Methodist minister named Hanson:

> I cannot say that I had a very distinct notion of what was required of me; but one thing I knew very well—I was wretched, and had no means of making myself otherwise. Moreover, I knew that I could pray for light… After this, I saw the world in a new light. I seemed to live in a new world, surrounded by new objects, and to be animated by new hopes and desires. I loved all mankind—slaveholders not excepted; though I abhorred slavery more than ever. My great concern was, now, to have the world converted.[52]

Several observations can be made. First, his religious convictions, or new affinity for religion, tempered his view of slaveholders as "a band of successful robbers." An awareness of his own wretchedness in the eyes of God and of the kindness of some slaveholders, convinced Douglass of the mutual degradation caused by slavery. Whites as well as blacks were wretched and in need of conversion. It was possible indeed to hate the sin but love the sinner.

This new awareness helped Douglass to lay hold of his loyalties. The universal need for reconciliation in Christ enabled Douglass to hold in tension his condition as a slave and his fondness for whites—like Daniel Lloyd, Lucretia Auld and Sophia Auld, all who treated him with kindness. Douglass remained vehemently opposed to slavery as an institution. By embracing faith in Jesus Christ, however, and by understanding slavery as part of a larger saga of human sinfulness, he softened his appraisal

---

[51] Douglass, *My Bondage and My Freedom*, 231.
[52] Ibid.

of white sympathizers. They too were harmed by the institution they defended.

As his hatred of slaveholders was changed by religion, so too his hatred of slavery was changed by his religious beliefs. Though no less adamant about emancipation, Douglass wrote that the zeal of his hatred for slavery became enlisted in a broader campaign for conversion. In other words, he accepted religious reasons for freedom beyond the personal reasons he entertained previously. Convinced that freedom was ordained by God, and that sinfulness obtained universally, Douglass came to believe that not only his enslavement but slavery as an institution needed to end. The upshot is that Douglass began to distinguish between a private ethic grounded in an "unofficial answer" to the morality of slavery and a public or social ethic. Douglass came to see that there was more at stake than his own freedom. Conversion confirmed for him that God intended freedom for all people; education provided him with a new and formal way to make the case.

For his part, Hanson helped Douglass to understand his story within a broader saga of redemption that judged sinfulness and championed freedom. Hanson, however, intended Douglass to understand that the freedom he preached was only a "spiritual freedom." Accordingly, equality between blacks and whites was a negative principle: black and white alike were sinners before God. In time, Douglass liberated this principle from its slaveholders' trappings and thought of freedom in a public and political way.

Interestingly, Douglass's sense of being deceived and cheated by slaveholders was not alleviated by his religious convictions. That was one sin Douglass seemed unable to forgive or forget. The hypocrisy of slaveholders who performed evil in the name of good always aroused Douglass's ardor.

Hanson brought Douglass to an understanding of the wretchedness of all people, and to the power of prayer. It was a black man named Lawson, however, who became Douglass's spiritual mentor. Though he was scarcely able to read, he taught Douglass the gospel. Douglass described him in resemblance and spirit as the very counterpart of Harriet Beecher Stowe's "Uncle Tom." [53]

> The good old man had told me, that the "Lord had a great work for me to do;" and I must prepare to do it; and that he had been shown that I must preach the gospel. His words made a deep impression on my mind, and I verily felt that some such work was before me, though I could not see how I should ever engage in its performance.... The advice and the suggestions of Uncle Lawson, were not without their influence upon my character and destiny. He threw my thoughts into a channel from which they have never entirely diverged. [54]

Lawson's assurances that Douglass would be useful in the world were welcomed by the younger man. Lawson inspired Douglass, and in his words Douglass found an incentive to continue hoping for deliverance from bondage. With this hope again enlivened, Douglass recommitted himself to his quest for knowledge. The notion that God had a purpose for him other than to be a slave enabled Douglass to enlist religion along with education in his quest for freedom. Having already learned how to read, he focused on learning how to write. This activity consumed his remaining time in Baltimore.

In March of 1833, at the age of fifteen, Douglass was removed from the Aulds and returned to the Eastern Shore. This time, however, Douglass was not returned to the Wye Plantation. He was sent instead to St. Michael's, to the service Hugh Auld's brother, Thomas. Douglass was acquainted with Thomas Auld as the husband of his master's daughter, Lucretia Anthony. Lucretia had since died and Thomas had remarried. Douglass was about to embark on what would become his darkest days in slavery.

He wrote of his service to Thomas and Rowena Auld: "I was made—for the first time in seven years—to feel the pinchings of

---

[53] Ibid., 243.
[54] Ibid., 233.

hunger."[55] Perhaps it owed to the Aulds's meanness in not giving their slaves enough to eat, but Douglass grew increasingly defiant in tone toward his new master and mistress. Curiously, Douglass was put to work as a house servant and spared the drudgery of life as a field hand. But even the life of a house servant paled in comparison to the relative freedom and comfort he had enjoyed in Baltimore.

This reversal of fortune not only changed Douglass's tone, but also his demeanor. He was not submissive, and even worse, he boldly defended himself against what he perceived to be his master's capricious complaints. Not even whippings changed his behavior. The slaveholder, for his part, was in the unenviable position of teaching a slave accustomed to privilege, long doted on, to accept his status and act like a slave.

Douglass's defiance also issued in a form of indirect resistance to his enslavement. Though he lacked the space to further his education, Douglass stole food from his master. He wrote that the three slaves who worked with him in the Big House were compelled "either to beg, or to steal..." Douglass treats the reader to a glimpse of his moral reasoning in defense of that stealing. He stated emphatically in his 1855 narrative (a point not found in the 1845 narrative) that taking food when he was hungry was not the mere result of an "unreasoning instinct," but "the result of a clear apprehension of the claims of morality."[56]

Douglass drew a sharp distinction between stealing from slaveholders and stealing from slaves. It was impossible, he reasoned, for a slave to steal from a master: "In the case of my master, it was only a question of removal—the taking his meat out of one tub, and putting it into another; the ownership of the meat was not affected by the transaction. At first, he owned it in the tub, and last, he owned it in me."[57]

Though his reasoning was antithetical to that preached to the slaves, he favored his own moral speculations on the matter to the

---

[55] Ibid., 246.
[56] Ibid., 246–47.
[57] Ibid., 247.

teachings of the slaveholding pulpit. Douglass, like other slaves, was not bound by the moral teachings of the slaveholders' church, choosing instead to think for himself on the matter while retaining his religious convictions. His moral thought in this instance is unique.

> I shall here make a profession of faith which may shock some, offend others, and be dissented from by all. It is this: Within the bounds of his just earnings, I hold that the slave is fully justified in helping himself to the *gold and silver, and the best apparel of his master, or that of any other slaveholder; and that such taking is not stealing in any just sense of that word.* The morality of free society can have no application to slave society. Slaveholders have made it almost impossible for the slave to commit any crime, known either to the laws of God or to the laws of man. If he steals, he takes his own; if he kills his master, he imitates only the heroes of the revolution. Slaveholders I hold to be individually and collectively responsible for all the evils which grow out of the horrid relation, and I believe they will be so held at the judgment, in the sight of a just God. Make a man a slave, and you rob him of moral responsibility. Freedom of choice is the essence of all accountability.[58]

Three important beliefs are here conjoined. First, stealing (or that which is commonly referred to as stealing) is permissible within certain parameters. Second, the morality of the free is not applicable to slave society. Third, slave behavior can be neither moral nor immoral. Moral responsibility cannot obtain without freedom of choice. These claims deserve further consideration.

Douglass referred to a "slave society," yet maintained that this society did not share in the morality of slaveholders. This leads one to the conclusion that slaves on a plantation lived within a discrete moral system. Next, however, he claimed that slaves had

---

[58] Ibid., 248.

no moral responsibility. If slaves had no moral responsibility, to what extent did they comprise a society? What then is the moral basis of their community? What were its defining beliefs? If, on the other hand, Douglass intended to argue that slaves had no moral responsibility vis-a-vis slaveholders, what did that mean for the slave community itself? Was it a discrete social community, competent to think morally, or did it acquiesce to the dominant slaveholding morality by its own moral inability? I believe that Douglass intended something akin to this correction: Slavery disallowed moral comity between slaves and slaveholders, and therefore disallowed the moral accountability of slaves to their masters. In other words, the biblical commandment "Thou shall not steal" established a moral duty for slaveholders and for slaves *within their respective communities*, but did not impose a moral obligation upon slaves to their masters.

Slaveholders, however, were caught in a moral conundrum. Unlike their human chattel, slaveholders enjoyed freedom of choice. Freedom, in turn, established an obligation to moral responsibility. By prosecuting slaves for crimes such as theft, slaveholders revealed twisted logic and dysfunctional moral judgment. They demanded slaves to be morally responsible *to whites*, though coercion and violence were normative practices. Conversely, slaveholders acknowledged no such responsibility to slaves, though they enjoyed freedom of choice. Hypocrisy, duplicity, and immunity were the cardinal compass points of slaveholding power.

Slaves resided in a culture and a community that reflected their understanding of the good. This culture was not removed from the larger slaveholding culture, but on the contrary rose in response to the abuses of the larger culture. Similarly, the morality of slave culture reflected the teachings of Christianity, but it screened-out the hypocrisy of slaveholding Christianity and made Christian tenets applicable to the lives of slaves.

Let us look at two examples of the moral standards within the slave culture. The first, described above, reflects a common understanding shared by slaves on the distinction between stealing and "taking." The second example reflects a common understanding shared by slaves on the faith claims of slaveholders.

Douglass did not argue that "taking" was a virtue or a sin. Rather, it was an amoral activity that turned on two broad appeals: to the logic of slavery and to God. First, appealing to the logic of slavery, how can property steal property? Slaveholders defended the contentious claims that their slaves, as property, held no legal rights. As persons, however, their slaves faced criminal prosecution and moral censure for violating the rights of whites. By what standard of justice can one be charged with violating the rights of others, who has not even the most basic right to possess determination of self? Douglass capitalized on this twisted reasoning by playing the devil's advocate and arguing the correct conclusion to the proposition: Slaves were property and held no rights. In that case, slaves were legally and morally absolved from the crime of theft against their masters. They could "take" from their masters, an amoral act, but they could not "steal" from those who held them as property. Douglass did not apply this argument to whites generally, but only to those whites who held slaves and to fellow slaves as well.

Douglass also appealed to God in this argument. He suggested that God's judgment on slavery and all the evils that it occasioned would fall squarely on slaveholders. They punished slaves for various offenses but disregarded their own culpability for the crime of slavery. God, however, was not blind to their crime and did not judge the victims of chattel slavery for the sins of its practitioners.

In the second case, there is evidence that slaves often judged slaveholders according to the moral standards of the slave culture. Take the matter of religious conversion. Slaves generally believed that slaveholders who truly accepted Christian teachings would emancipate their slaves. Thus, "The highest evidence the slaveholder can give the slave of his acceptance with God, is the emancipation of his slaves. This is proof that he is willing to give up all to God, and for the sake of God. Not to do this, was, in my estimation, and in the opinion of all the slaves, an evidence of half-heartedness, and wholly inconsistent with the idea of genuine conversion."[59] The theological beliefs of slaves, while influenced by slaveholding religion, reflected their own interpretation of the slaves social location and addressed their own needs.

For his part, Douglass found half-heartedness in the later conversion of Master Thomas. "If religion had any effect on his character at all," Douglass wrote, "it made him more cruel and hateful in all his ways."[60] Thomas Auld's post-conversion disposition strengthened Douglass's observation that "Southern" religion was a sham.

If religion made Auld more brutal toward his slaves, it made Douglass more bitter. By the time he wrote his first autobiography in 1845, Douglass had no kind words for "Southern" religion. He drew a distinction between it and legitimate Christianity. Douglass's overall lack of enthusiasm for organized religion, however, suggests that his religious beliefs were tempered with his own moral formulations and speculations about God.

The advances and gains in treatment that Douglass experienced in Baltimore over the course of seven years were, in nine months time, negated and replaced with the "bitterest dregs of slavery" under the brutal treatment of farmer Edward Covey.[61] This reversal of fortune, coupled with his growing frustration at the vacuity of religion, made Douglass prone to outbursts. The year spent with Covey marked a dramatic turning point in Douglass's life. During this time Douglass determined that the man who succeeded in whipping him would also succeed in killing him. Douglass's defiance did not arise *ex nihilo*. Rather, the seeds of his reaction to Covey were sown as a boy in Tuckahoe and tended in the relative mildness of Baltimore. That his indirect resistance to slavery blossomed into rebellion during his service to Covey has much to do with the new and increasing cruelty of his circumstances. Douglass's strong sense of self, moral beliefs, and aspiration enabled him to refine a credo from the dross of his misery: the young Douglass would not be shackled. He had to

---

[59] Ibid., 251.

[60] Ibid., 252.

[61] Douglass, *Narrative of the Life of Frederick Douglass*, 58.

endure the most horrific six months of his life to establish this creedal self-affirmation.

THE COVEY EXPERIENCE

No doubt Thomas Auld grew tired of Douglass's demeanor. The strapping youth was all but useless on a farm. Auld's remedy was to hire out Douglass for a year to a man some seven miles away with a reputation for breaking slaves of their rebellious spirits. Edward Covey's reputation was well deserved: "Mr. Covey succeeded in breaking me. I was broken in body, soul, and spirit. My natural elasticity was crushed, my intellect languished, the disposition to read departed, the cheerful spark that lingered about my eye died; the dark night of slavery closed in upon me; and behold a man transformed into a brute."[62]

The "dark night" of Douglass's slavery commenced 1 January 1834. Douglass was not quite sixteen years old. For the first six months of that year, he was whipped virtually every week. He was worked to the limits of endurance every day. The constant work, often accompanied by the lash, was successful in taming Douglass. He had neither the space necessary for moral reflection nor the leisure to read. He contemplated suicide. Douglass had come too far to comply with such servitude. He imagined that either suicide or escape were his best options. The cruelty of Covey's treatment diminished Douglass's fear of death. Although neither Covey nor Douglass knew it then, this was the final ingredient necessary for Douglass to overcome his bondage. His indirect resistance to bondage through education was not possible in the field. His protestations about mistreatment went unheard. His prayers were labored, spoken with the misconception that God would spare him the misery of service under Covey. Driven by increasing despondency, Douglass finally erupted into violent self-defense on an occasion when Covey thought to administer the

---

[62] Ibid.

routine of brutal punishment for the slave's alleged neglect of duty.

The beginnings of Douglass's ultimate outright rebellion occurred one afternoon when his strength failed and he passed out. Learning of the young slave's condition, Covey responded violently. He kicked Douglass several times while he lay on the ground. Suspecting Douglass feigned ill health, Covey took a hickory slat and struck him on the head, causing a large wound. Douglass made no effort to comply with Covey's demands that he get up, resolving instead to let Covey do his worst.

After a time, when Douglass's health rebounded, he stole away the seven miles to St. Michael's and sought his master's protection from Covey. This latest injustice was too extreme for Douglass to bear in silence. He appealed to Auld, hoping for compassion. Auld rejected Douglass's plea for protection from Covey and for a new home. He was told to return to Covey the next day. Douglass returned on a Sabbath to find Covey remarkably unperturbed over the slave's unauthorized absence. On the following Monday morning, however, Covey appeared to punish the slave. Douglass refused to be punished and fought back. The two squared-off in a stable. "Mr. Covey seemed now to think he had me, and could do what he pleased; but at this moment—from whence came the spirit I don't know—I resolved to fight; and suiting my action to the resolution, I seized Covey hard by the throat; and as I did so, I rose."[63] The fight lasted a long time, Douglass estimated it's duration at about two hours. Covey called for help from other slaves, but to no avail. Douglass recorded with satisfaction in his 1855 autobiography that Covey feigned victory but actually "gave up the contest."[64]

After the battle, little changed between the two in one sense, but in another, everything had changed. Douglass returned to work in accordance with Covey's orders. His servitude had not changed, but his sense of self blossomed into maturity. "This battle with Mr. Covey was the turning point in my career as a slave. It rekindled

---

[63] Ibid., 64.

[64] Douglass, *My Bondage and My Freedom*, 285.

the few expiring embers of freedom, and revived within me a
sense of my own manhood. It recalled the departed self-
confidence, and inspired me again with a determination to be
free."[65] During the next six months with Covey, and for the
duration of his following four years in slavery, Douglass was
never again whipped. Bold defiance turned suicidal thoughts into
notions of escape.

Although a boon to his ego, Douglass's battle with Covey
weakened his dependence upon God. His treatment at the hands of
Covey cast doubt in his mind about all religion.[66] His prayers were
feigned, for he believed that only a sham God could be at the
receiving end of the sham religion that prevailed around him. The
Covey experience led him "to the conviction that prayers were
unavailing and delusive."[67] His resolve, and not prayerful religion,
informed his defiance. "My religious views on the subject of
resisting my master had suffered a serious shock, by the savage
persecution to which I had been subjected, and my hands were no
longer tied by my religion."[68]

Douglass's religious thought took a significant turn from his
days in Baltimore. Then, he needed God's protection and gui-
dance. Suffering under Covey, however, caused Douglass to revise
his estimates of God's providence and the efficacy of worship. His
statement, "my hands were no longer tied by my religion," aptly
expressed his change of mind. He still revered God, but more so
now as a philosophical "first principle" than as personal savior.
Douglass did not push God offstage, but God no longer occupied
center stage in his life. On the subject of abolition, for example,
Douglass believed freedom to be both a divine aim and a human
project. Douglass did not doubt that God willed freedom as an
eternal aim, but he credited human resolve with the proximate
manifestations of freedom. Human effort was the material cause of
freedom. The upshot for his religious thought was that Douglass
was no longer content to wait upon God to do for him what his

---

[65] Douglass, *Narrative of the Life of Frederick Douglass*, 65.
[66] Douglass, *My Bondage and My Freedom*, 278.
[67] Ibid.
[68] Ibid., 282.

effort could accomplish. On the contrary, Douglass believed that God worked through such efforts. To be free, then, Douglass needed a good plan more than fervent prayer.

ESCAPE ATTEMPT

The thought of being only a creature of the present and the past troubled me, and I longed to have a future—a future with hope in it. To be shut up entirely to the past and present is to the soul whose life and happiness is unceasing progress—what the prison is to the body—a blight and a mildew, a hell of horrors.[69]

His year with Covey left Douglass a creature of the present and the past. Preoccupied with survival, with getting through the day unscathed, Douglass was committed to die in self-defense if necessary. But he had no plan to better his condition and little hope that he could do so while in service to Covey. When his contractual year with Covey was concluded, Thomas Auld hired Douglass out to another Eastern Shore planter. January 1835 found Douglass bound for a new home and a new overseer. William Freeland, unlike Covey, was a gentleman. He was open, mild, and frank. At Freeland's farm, Douglass's condition was vastly improved. Freeland gave his slaves time to eat meals, and time to themselves after sundown when the daily work ceased. The material amenities notwithstanding, Douglass was restless and discontented. He grew impatient with his servitude and, unlike most other slaves, refused even to appear contented. Experience taught Douglass that one's fortunes as a slave were easily reversed. Obedience and disobedience did not correlate con-sistently to favorable and unfavorable treatment.

For a literate, thoughtful, and strong-willed slave like Douglass, mild treatment correlated positively with resistance. He knew that as long as he was a slave, he would always be

---

[69] Douglass, *Life and Times*, 604.

vulnerable to the threat of worse treatment, a threat to keep his aspirations for freedom and defiance in check. He knew that as long as he was a slave he could not aspire to a meaningful future. On the contrary, he would have to repress any hope at all for a meaningful future. Douglass knew as well that God would not mount any supernatural rescue effort to free him. To be free, he would have to strike the blow himself. Douglass understood clearly the choice that was before him. He could choose to accommodate himself to his present condition and surroundings, or he could choose to hope for a meaningful future and act on what that choice implied. The options were mutually exclusive. As an institution, slavery replaced any hope the slave entertained for a meaningful future with fear of a perilous future. The move to Freeland's farm afforded Douglass the space to take stock of his situation and he chose to project a meaningful future for himself as a freeman.

Douglass's decision to throw off slavery was possible because of his prior moral commitments and because he learned a thing or two about the morality of slavery. First and foremost, Douglass intended to embrace a full sense of self and to act in accordance with his own wishes. Douglass committed himself to being an independent moral agent and to ordering his own values. Douglass was also committed to self-betterment through learning and reflection. Education and contemplation were his chief assets. They gave him the wherewithal to underscore the inner-logic of slavery as an immoral system, and grounded his case for freedom in a fundamental and inalienable human right: the God-given right to be free. Lastly, Douglass committed himself to self-defense. He refused to be whipped without protest, and in overcoming his fear of the lash, he took an important step toward freedom. Fear of a perilous future no longer restrained his aspirations. Douglass's commitment to self-defense held religious and moral significance. He believed that religion in the South was largely a pretext used to justify slavery and that waiting upon God for deliverance apart from acting on the desire was a formula for complacency.

Douglass was an excellent student of slavery. His insights into the slave system informed his resolve to be free. Douglass learned the "standard morality"[70] of slavery. Contrary to the themes of paternal benevolence and obedience to God's will that the slaveholding pulpit preached to slaves, Douglass observed the ways slavery undermined the humanity of slaves. And he learned how slaves fought back.

The standard morality of slavery claimed among its favored tenets: ignorance was virtue, family meaningless, personal responsibility nil, no beginnings were to be made in the world, no future held promises of qualitative change, one's fate was wholly arbitrary, no meaningful sense of self could be cultivated, and no civilization was meant to flourish among Africans. Marriage was jeopardized and fidelity to one's mate was supererogatory. There was no incentive for slaves to lead a holy life; they could fear God, but they had to revere absolute and irresponsible power. Reason was imprisoned and passion was encouraged to run wild. The abuse of alcohol was encouraged during the Christmas vacation period. During his bouts of disbelief, Douglass ultimately affirmed that only a sham god could intend such "moral" teachings as the rubric of right living.

In contrast to the "standard morality" of slavery, Douglass learned moral lessons from the slave community: Though slavery could keep civilization at bay, it did not eliminate human nature. Douglass believed that there was a substantial self existing beneath the nameless face of the slave—a self that was imbued with the inalienable rights that divine providence granted humanity. Her humanity could be degraded to unimaginable depths, but the slave's humanity could not be eradicated. And where there was a trace of humanity, there was hope that slaves could be restored to well being.

The noteworthy development of 1835, his first year in service to Freeland, was his attachment to other slaves. Douglass started an underground Sunday school and devoted many of his evenings to educating fellow slaves. He taught slaves how to read the Bible. He also instructed them in the abolitionist arguments he memorized from *The Columbian Orator*. According to Douglass,

---

[70] Douglass, *My Bondage and My Freedom*, 176.

his public speaking activities began here.[71] Two slaves in particular became Douglass's dearest friends, brothers Henry and John Harris. They were the only slaves owned by Freeland. Three others, Sandy Jenkins, Handy Caldwell, and Douglass himself, were hired out to Freeland. Douglass took particular interest in the Harris brothers, and sought to imbue them with his own thinking and outlook on slavery and abolition. He felt for the first time a deep-seated responsibility toward fellow slaves. Their condition was inextricably connected to his own. Douglass described his love for Henry and John Harris as the strongest love he ever experienced.

Douglass's attachment to fellow slaves reveals an important development in his moral thought. Prior to this point, Douglass entertained notions of freedom for himself and grounded those notions in an abolitionist argument on the God-given and inalienable right of human freedom. Douglass taught from this perspective. His appeal to scripture was an exercise in liberation theology. It was contextual, it was committed to the full humanity of black people, it endorsed the view that God intended for blacks to be free, and it issued in an act of liberation. For these reasons, the "Sunday school" remained underground and was implicated in a runaway plot.

Given his love for Henry and John, and given his resolve to become his own master, it comes as no surprise that Douglass included the two men in his "life-giving determination" to secure liberty.[72] The men planned an escape that was foiled by another slave. That the escape attempt was unsuccessful does not diminish its importance in Douglass's narrative. For his part in the escape attempt, Douglass could have been sent to the deep South, a move which would have in all probability crippled his resolve to escape and crushed his hopes for freedom. Circumstance could have trumped his intentionality and trapped him in the unending misery of slavery. As it happened, however Thomas Auld decided against sending Douglass to the deep South and decided instead to send

---

[71] Douglass, *Life and Times*, 605.
[72] Douglass, *Narrative of the Life of Frederick Douglass*, 73.

his young, defiant slave back to Baltimore to learn a trade. After an absence of three years, Douglass returned to Baltimore, back to the home of Hugh and Sophia Auld. His attempt at escape was punished by sending him closer to freedom's door.

Back in Baltimore, Douglass learned ship-building skills and was trusted eventually to hire himself out. His proficiency as a caulker earned Douglass top wages and made him an asset to his master. Douglass sought employment, made contracts and collected his earnings as did free men. As a slave, though, he turned his earnings—up to nine dollars a week—over to Hugh Auld. The injustice of the arrangement was too much for Douglass to bear and he searched for avenues of escape. Hugh Auld's warnings against escape fell upon deaf ears. "He exhorted me to content myself... if I would be happy, I must lay out no plans for the future."[73] Plans for the future, however, motivated Douglass to work hard and kept his spirits high. Living in Baltimore once again only fueled Douglass's yearning for freedom.

I have observed this in my experience of slavery—that whenever my condition was improved, instead of its increasing my contentment, it only increased my desire to be free, and set me to thinking of plans to gain my freedom. I have found that, to make a contented slave, it is necessary to make a thoughtless one. It is necessary to darken his moral and mental vision, and, as far as possible, to annihilate the power of reason. He must be able to detect no inconsistencies in slavery; he must be made to feel that slavery is right; and he can be brought to that only when he ceases to be a man.[74]

Reason, resolve, moral and mental vision, hope for a meaningful future, these are the qualities that make for a discontented slave, a slave who is apt to rebel. Interestingly, at no point in this excerpt does Douglass mention God. The power of

---

[73] Ibid., 86.
[74] Ibid., 83–84.

reason and not the power of God is the final arbiter of freedom. Freedom falls within the domain of "manhood"; it bears God's image, and affirms God's will for humanity, but it is obtained by the dint of human effort.

On 3 September 1838, Douglass dealt a mortal blow to his servitude and escaped to New York. His twenty-year sojourn in slavery had ended. His escape vindicated the idea that divine and human forces interact to forge an individual's destiny; the cooperation of divine providence and human agency were established. Douglass's conclusion on the cooperation of divine providence and human agency ended an internal debate that troubled him for years. During times of relative ease and comfort, such as his seven-year tenure in Baltimore, Douglass affirmed that God did not ordain slavery but freedom. Under more oppressive conditions, such as the first six months with Covey, Douglass questioned whether God intended for his enslavement and this idea led him to doubt God's existence.

Curiously, Douglass credited "manly independence," not God, for his successful resistance to Covey. He wrote, "After resisting him, I felt as I had never felt before. It was a resurrection from the dark and pestiferous tomb of slavery, to the heaven of comparative freedom."[75] Douglass affirmed that freedom was secured by dint of courageous human action. The chain of doubt weighed heavily on Douglass for the three years between his rebellion and escape. He debated whether to place his trust in God or "manly courage."[76] With liberty attained, the matter was settled. Douglass credited both God and human agency for his success: "The contest was now ended; the chain was severed; God and right stood vindicated. I was a freeman."[77]

Having achieved freedom, Douglass did not believe God intended that only he and a relative few others among all enslaved Africans should enjoy freedom. On the contrary, his experience in slavery induced him to reflect on God's will for blacks, and on the

---

[75] Douglass, *My Bondage and My Freedom*, 286.

[76] Ibid., 350.

[77] Ibid.

will of blacks to be free. The opportunity to address abolitionists a few years after his escape was appealing to Douglass in part because he could see himself, if only dimly at this point, in the role of exemplar. This discussion, however, awaits the next chapter.

3

The Garrisonian Episode

Introduction

As it is in physics, so in morals, there are cases which demand irritation and counter irritation. The con-science of the American public needs this irritation. And I would blister it all over, from centre to circumference, until it gives signs of a purer and a better life than it is now manifesting to the world.[1]

For ten turbulent years, stretching from 1841 to 1851, Frederick Douglass brought the question of American slavery before the conscience of the American public with unrivaled ferocity and persuasiveness. As an agent of the Massachusetts Anti-Slavery Society, and as a devout follower of William Lloyd Garrison, Douglass was indefatigable in his polemic against American slavery.

---

[1] Frederick Douglass, quoted in Philip Foner, ed. *The Life and Writings of Frederick Douglass* (New York: International Publishers, 1950) 1:237.

From the time he captured Garrison's attention at an anti-slavery convention in Nantucket during the summer of 1841, until his contentious break with the Garrisonians a decade later, Douglass was the lion of the Garrisonian circuit. Gaining extensive notoriety from a tour of the British Empire between 1845 and 1847, Douglass returned to the United States a nationally known figure. Over the course of the next four years, he toured the country as a committed Garrisonian, engaging the public with a power and a charm that commanded the attention and respect of even his most ardent foes. The Garrisonian episode in Douglass's life is marked by two distinct periods: (a) 1841–1847, the years prior to the founding of the *North Star* in December 1847; and, (b) 1847–1851, the years prior to Douglass's break from the Garrisonians, during which he combined editing his own newspaper with lecturing on behalf of the Garrisonians.

THE EARLY YEARS

Shortly after arriving at New Bedford, Douglass was introduced to Garrison's abolitionist paper, the *Liberator*, which became Douglass's inspiration and made Garrison a hero to Douglass's mind. Douglass wrote in his memoirs that Garrison's paper "took its place with me next to the Bible."[2] Beyond inspiring Douglass, and beyond the paper's ability to put into words many of Douglass's convictions, the *Liberator* exposed Douglass to the principles of the antislavery movement.[3] He wrote, "I had already the spirit of the movement, and only needed to understand its principles and measures."[4] The principles of Garrisonian abolitionism were new to him, but he was certainly familiar with the general arguments for abolition.

---

[2] Frederick Douglass, *My Bondage and My Freedom* (New York, 1855), in Henry Louis Gates, Jr., ed. *Frederick Douglass/Autobiographies* (New York: Library of America/Penguin Books, 1994) 362.
[3] Ibid., 363.
[4] Ibid.

Garrison's *Liberator* became a central factor in Douglass's intellectual development for several reasons. The paper vehemently denounced slavery, bringing to light the hypocrisy of those engaged in the "peculiar institution." It "preached human brotherhood, denounced oppression," and demanded the complete and immediate emancipation of all the slaves.[5] The *Liberator* corroborated Douglass's own convictions about slavery.

Douglass greatly admired Garrison because his words were few, to the point, and saturated with fiery indignation. Further, as Douglass pointed out about himself, he was "something of a hero worshiper by nature."[6] To an escaped slave with a fondness for heroic characters, Garrison was made to order. Though Douglass exaggerated when he described the spontaneous feelings of his heart toward Garrison in the words, "you are the man, the Moses raised up by God, to deliver his modern Israel from bondage," no doubt Garrison's commitment to the liberation of slaves deeply impressed Douglass.[7]

Garrisonianism was significant to Douglass for another reason as well. In 1838 Garrison's wing of the abolitionist movement, the American Anti-Slavery Society, had no direct competition in New Bedford. Douglass favored Garrisonian abolitionism because it was highly-charged, aggressive in outreach, and uncontested. The American and Foreign Anti-Slavery Society, opposed to Garrisonian abolitionism, did not form until 1840.

For at least two years, Douglass bonded with Garrison's brand of abolition, and moreover, he bonded with Garrison. Had the American and Foreign Anti-Slavery Society competed for Douglass's loyalty, it is not at all clear that Douglass would have preferred the Garrisonian movement. In the absence of competition, Douglass's loyalty to Garrison grew without challenge.

Garrisonian abolitionism gave primacy to several moral tenets. First, Garrison defended moral suasion to the exclusion of political action. Moral suasion was a religious duty for Garrison,

---

[5] Ibid., 362.
[6] Ibid.
[7] Ibid.

not merely a political expedient. It was a pillar of sorts, supporting Garrison's system and establishing a strong moral foundation for the movement. Nonresistance was the other religious pillar that supported Garrison's system. Interestingly, though Garrison was an advocate for peace, he believed that the use of force was at times appropriate. "Rather than see men wearing their chains in a cowardly and servile spirit, I would, as an advocate of peace, rather see them breaking the head of the tyrant with their chains."[8] Although nonresistance was preferable to physical resistance, Garrison understood that the use of force indicated "a positive sign of moral growth."[9] At the very least, the use of force in self-defense indicated that one had a self to defend and the intention to press one's claims over against the arbitrary and absolute power of slaveholders. His views on the use of force, however, did not diminish his commitment to nonresistance. Together, moral suasion and nonresistance planted Garrisonian abolitionism firmly in New Testament ethics.

Garrison demanded the immediate, complete, and unconditional emancipation of all slaves. Further, Garrison did not endorse the recolonization of slaves in Africa. He was, on the contrary, an early integrationist who recognized the direct correlation between racism and the perpetuation of slavery.

Garrison advocated "disunionism" as the political corollary to the demand for immediate emancipation. "No union with slaveholders" was one of his most repeated rallying cries. Unlike some abolitionists who heard in the cry, "No *Christian* union with slaveholders," meaning that slaveholders ought to be expelled from the church for infidelity, Garrison intended *neither* Christian nor political union with slaveholders. Such a union would only serve to vitiate the superior moral position of non-slaveholders. As a result, Garrison implored his followers and all Christians to come out of the proslavery church and, ultimately, to come out of the proslavery union.

---

[8] William Lloyd Garrison, quoted in George M. Fredrickson, *The Inner Civil War* (New York: Harper and Row, 1965), 42.
  [9] Ibid., 42.

Disunionism was undergirded by Garrison's belief that the US Constitution was essentially and irrevocably a slaveholding document. His proslavery interpretation of the Constitution disallowed any political compromise with slaveholders; it therefore rendered political action futile at best and self-defeating at worst. Garrison even denounced basic modes of political expression such as voting. The rejection of the Constitution and of the union itself were necessary if the slaves were to be freed. Anything less than the total rejection of the Constitution and the union would fail to extirpate the evil of slavery from the land once and for all. Had Garrison endorsed an antislavery interpretation of the Constitution, disunionism might not have been a necessity; and political action might have seemed a viable course of action. For Garrison, however, the nation was not only corrupt in practice, but it was also corrupt in its most basic expression of union. Slavery corrupted the American mind so completely that the only alternative was to start over again. Though Garrison defended the position admirably, in time not even enthusiasts like Douglass were willing to end the American experiment and start over again. There was simply no evidence that such an outcome would be beneficial to the slaves. Douglass came to believe that dissolving the union and dissolving slavery were not synonymous. Theoretically, the latter could occur without requiring the former.

Given his experiences as a slave and his admiration of Garrison, it is not difficult to understand why Douglass became a committed Garrisonian. His commitment, however, was not devoid of tension and even disagreement. While several Garrisonian tenets were congruent with Douglass's beliefs, he affirmed others only halfheartedly, and rejected at least one tenet. Garrison's exhortation to come out of the proslavery church was congruent with Douglass's perception of the Southern church as professing a sham religion. Similarly, Garrison's observation that anti-negro prejudice made slavery respectable was confirmed by Douglass's experiences.

Garrison's beliefs in favor of moral suasion, of disunionism, and of the Constitution as a proslavery document, were affirmed by Douglass only halfheartedly. In the years following, Douglass took exception to each of these beliefs. But in the early 1840s he defended them in accordance with the standards of the American Anti-Slavery Society. Douglass was sympathetic to the argument for moral suasion on Christian grounds, for example, but he was not an eager advocate. As for disunionism and Garrison's proslavery interpretation of the US Constitution, there is no evidence that Douglass was either inclined or disinclined to such positions before his exposure to the *Liberator*. One can maintain minimally that Douglass saw the logic of these proposals and defended them, due largely to his respect for Garrison's project.

Douglass rejected only one of the Garrisonian tenets in his early years as a member of Garrison's movement. Nonresistance offended Douglass's fighting spirit. The man who fought his overseer and who believed that "he who was whipped easiest was whipped oftenest," did not allow himself to be pummeled by hostile audiences without defending himself. John Blassingame was correct; Douglass was nonviolent during his first years on the antislavery circuit, but abandoned the practice in the fall of 1843 when he was attacked by a mob in Pendleton, Indiana.[10]

Waldo Martin contends that Douglass did not accept Garrison's doctrine of nonresistance because he found it lofty and impractical.[11] I agree with Martin's assessment, but add that Douglass's problem with nonresistance had as much to do with his fighting spirit as with the practicality of nonresistance.

James McPherson states that Douglass did not accept nonresistance because "retaliatory violence against the white man had a cleansing and lifting effect on the spirit, and seemed to bring about a psychological if not physical emancipation from the intolerable tensions of submission."[12] I agree with McPherson in part. No doubt Douglass found psychological emancipation in resisting Covey. Yet, he did not advocate retaliatory violence

---

[10] *The Frederick Douglass Papers*, ed. John W. Blassingame et al. 5 vols. (New York: Yale University Press, 1979) 1:xliii.

[11] Waldo Martin, *The Mind of Frederick Douglass* (Chapel Hill: University of North Carolina Press, 1984) 23–24.

[12] Benjamin Quarles, *Frederick Douglass*, foreword by James McPherson (New York: Atheneum, repr. 1968).

because he correctly understood its futility. While the individual could decide for herself to resist violently and to risk death, retaliatory violence did not make good policy. Douglass understood that there were times when it was necessary to refrain from retaliation. Resistance, on the other hand, was always in season, and took a multitude of forms.

Beyond the influence of his teachings, Garrison can also be credited with exposing Douglass to American and European audiences, access to influential abolitionists, and a forum within which to hone his oratorical skills and to speak his mind. Each of these items proved indispensable to Douglass's success as the foremost representative of the slaves, and to the formulation of his mature thought.

By endorsing Garrison's precepts and by rethinking those precepts in light of the lessons he learned as a slave and now as a freeman, Douglass isolated and clarified his own convictions. In this way, Garrison provided Douglass with a benchmark of sorts, a developed system of belief against which to measure, or compare his own beliefs. This was Garrison's greatest gift. Ever the student, Douglass gained some analytic clarity and some political insights from his Garrisonian friends and mentors.

THE MORAL AGENDA

Douglass wrote in his second autobiographical account that, at the behest of fellow Garrisonians, he curtailed his desire to "denounce" the wrongs of slavery and limited himself merely to "narrating" those wrongs. During his first three or four months on the lecture circuit, Douglass's speeches were "almost exclusively made up of narrations."[13] The activity grew tiresome day after day, month after month, and became "too mechanical" for Douglass to continue indefinitely.

Douglass found that his fellow abolitionists, although well-intentioned, discouraged him from "growing" and failed to

---

[13] Douglass, *My Bondage and My Freedom*, 367.

recognize that he "needed room."[14] While it may be true that Garrison and the Garrisonians endeavored to reign Douglass in to some extent, the speeches of record from that period do not bear out his claim that he stuck only to narrating wrongs. On the contrary, the speeches indicate that Douglass denounced the wrongs of slavery from the very beginning of his career.[15] Douglass struck a compromise of sorts; one that became characteristic of his lectures. He did not stick to the narrative exclusively, neither did he abandon the narrative in making a case for abolition. He used his narrative to accomplish an agenda: to engage his audiences, to set a context for his arguments, and to illustrate his points. Instead of centering on his personal narrative, he focused increasingly on moral and religious themes, thus putting his narrative to use as a pedagogical device. In this manner, Douglass used his story line to inform audiences about the reality of slavery and to drive home a broader moral point.

In an 1841 address delivered in Lynn, Massachusetts, for example, Douglass went beyond mere description of his experiences in slavery. At one point in the address, while relaying an experience as a slave in which he read a speech by John Quincy Adams to his fellow slaves, Douglass noted, "emancipation, my friends, is that cure for slavery and its evils. It alone will give to the South peace and quietness."[16]

Later in the same address, Douglass proclaimed, "prejudice against color is stronger north than south; it hangs around my neck like a heavy weight." Beyond mere narration, Douglass spoke his mind. In an address given the following month, Douglass told the northern crowd in attendance that the bulwark of slavery was constituted by the pledge of the north to return runaway slaves.[17] As a fugitive slave himself, Douglass made a strong appeal to his audience. He could be returned to slavery. Nevertheless, his focus

---

[14] Ibid.

[15] Blassingame, *The Frederick Douglass Papers*, 1:liii.

[16] Douglass (October 1841), quoted in Blassingame, *The Frederick Douglass Papers*, 1:4..

[17] Douglass (4 November 1841), quoted in Blassingame, *The Frederick Douglass Papers*, 1:6.

lay elsewhere. Douglass did not shy away from holding his audience responsible for its complicity in slavery.

Douglass had any number of ways available to him to impress audiences, and he approached his topic from a variety of perspectives. At times he made general observations about the nature of slavery in the United States. On other occasions he pursued a specific angle: the role of white racial prejudice in perpetuating slavery; the role of black resistance in abolishing slavery; the role of international pressure in bringing social reform to American shores; and, the efficacy of divine order and natural law arguments for abolition. His text depended largely upon his audience.

A working definition of slavery was the first order of business as Douglass entered into his speaking and publishing career. It became necessary when Douglass traveled to England, Ireland, and Scotland after the publication of his first autobiographical account in 1845. While in England, Douglass discovered among the people that it was common practice to refer to virtually every unpleasant experience—from drunkenness to hard work—as slavery. The practice threatened to trivialize the wrongs of American slavery. Speaking in London on 22 May 1846, Douglass defined American slavery:

> Slavery in the United States is the granting of that power by which one man exercises and enforces a right of property in the body and soul of another. The condition of a slave is simply that of the brute beast. He is a piece of property—a marketable commodity in the language of the law, to be bought or sold at the will and caprice of the master... His own good, his conscience, his intellect, his affections are all set aside by the master.[18]

In distinguishing American slavery from the more colloquial usage of the term, Douglass indicated what he found to be the

---

[18] Douglass (22 May 1846), quoted in Blassingame, *The Frederick Douglass Papers*, 1:273.

most egregious features of slavery. Instead of arguing the legality of slavery, Douglass chose to focus on the deprivation of goods. By arguing that the slave is deprived of basic goods—among these access to education, marriage protected by law, and self-determination—Douglass hoped to appeal to the conscience of his audience. This argument is consistent with his commitment to moral suasion. An advocate of political action might have appealed to the letter of the Constitution in an attempt to demonstrate that the Federal government was not acting in accordance with the liberties defended in the Constitution. Such a move might entail rebellion, if it could be successfully argued that the Federal government had lost its mandate. Douglass, however, avoided political discussions and pressed the moral case against slavery.

Similarly, when discussing the prospects for abolition, Douglass discounted even the possibility of legal recourse or of outright physical rebellion and argued at length for Garrison's strategy. In a transcription of an address delivered in New York City, Douglass reasoned that the slave had few viable options. "The anti-slavery movement is the only earthly hope of the American slave... there [is] no hope for the slave in church, or state, or in the working of society, framed as it now is; nothing whatever in any of the institutions of the day."[19]

Douglass cast both the problem of American slavery and its solution in moral terms. He believed that only those institutions that did not make concessions to slavery were fit to perform the work of establishing the divine goods denied by slavery. The popular political and religious institutions of the day, therefore, were ill suited to the task. By focusing on the moral case against slavery, and by dismissing the political case, Douglass defended Garrisonian abolitionism as the only sure way to end slavery.

Beyond a direct, moral assault on the institution of slavery, Douglass discussed the necessity of purging the nation of racial prejudice. White racial prejudice fueled the "peculiar institution"

---

[19] Douglass, (9 May 1843), quoted in Blassingame, *The Frederick Douglass Papers*, 1:21.

but received little scrutiny from white commentators. A typical demonstration of white racial prejudice focused on the hypocrisy of the perpetrators. Douglass very often relied upon humor or sarcasm to drive home the point, but the point remained virtually unchanged during his tenure as a lecturer. In establishing and maintaining slavery, whites created a system that systematically denied blacks the ability to be self-reliant and the opportunity for self-improvement, yet these same proslavery forces charged blacks with being inferior for their lack of achievement. Speaking before an audience of abolitionists and antislavery sympathizers in Massachusetts in December 1841, Douglass took his hosts to task:

> People in general will say they like colored men as well as any other, but in their proper place! They assign us that place; they don't let us do it for ourselves, nor will they allow us a voice in the decision. They will not allow that we have a head to think, and a heart to feel, and a soul to aspire. They treat us not as men, but as dogs—they cry "Stu-boy!" and expect us to run and do their bidding. That's the way we are liked. You degrade us, and then ask why we are degraded—you shut our mouths, and then ask why we don't speak—you close your colleges and seminaries against us, and then ask why we don't know more.[20]

This aspect of slavery, although not as overtly cruel and inhuman as the whippings, was equally pernicious in Douglass's eyes. Degradation inflicted as serious a wound as the lash.

Douglass often tailored the message to rebut the claims of opponents. In this excerpt from an article for the *Liberty Bell*, written in 1845, Douglass showed how hypocrisy and dishonesty infected statements made by the Reverend Orville Dewey, a

---

[20] Douglass, in an address titled "The Church and Prejudice" delivered at the Plymouth Church Anti-Slavery Society, December, 1841, quoted in Foner, *The Life and Writings of Frederick Douglass*, 1:104.

Unitarian minister and member of the American Colonization Society.

> When they tell the world that the Negro is ignorant, and naturally and intellectually incapacitated to appreciate and enjoy freedom, they also publish their own condemnation, by bringing to light those infamous laws by which the slave is compelled to live in grossest ignorance. When they tell the world that the slave is immoral, vicious and degraded, they but invite attention to their depravity: for the world sees the slave stripped, by his accusers, of every safeguard to virtue, even of that purest and most sacred institution of marriage. When they represent the slave as being destitute of religious principle...they profit nothing by the plea. In addition to their moral condemnation they brand themselves with bold and daring impiety, in making it an offense punishable with fine and imprisonment, and even death, to teach a slave to read the will of God.... When they attempt to shield themselves by the grossly absurd and wicked pretense that the slave is contented and happy, and, therefore "better off" in slavery than he could be possessed of freedom, their shield is broken by that long and bloody list of advertisements for runaway slaves who have left their happy homes, and sought for freedom, even at the hazard of losing their lives in the attempt to gain it.... And when, to cap the climax, Dr. Dewey tells the people of England that the white and colored people in this country are separated by an "impassable barrier," the hundreds of thousands of mulattoes, quadroons, etc. in this country, silently but unequivocally brand him with the guilt of having uttered a most egregious falsehood.[21]

---

[21] Douglass, quoted in Foner, *The Life and Writings of Frederick Douglass*, 1:114.

Beyond demonstrating how Douglass communicated the hypocrisy and prejudice of whites, this quote successfully captures a style of argumentation that contemporary biographers refer to as Douglass's irrefutable logic. Under Douglass, logic, sarcasm, humor, and a touch of black preaching were combined to form a most compelling method of argumentation.

The rhetoric notwithstanding, Douglass skillfully strengthened his polemic against slavery by amplifying the root causes in the perpetuation of slavery. More than a legal system that held blacks in bondage, slavery was also a school of thought that relied heavily upon false assumptions, flawed evidence, and sophistic reasoning. Proslavery advocates made slavery appear reasonable, practical, and moral. Douglass attacked slavery, in part, by challenging its reliance upon flawed conceptions of blacks, conceptions which bespoke white prejudice and not black inferiority. This attack undercut the claims of sympathy by Northern whites. Douglass revealed their complicity and duplicity in the slave trade.

The role of black resistance in abolishing slavery was another of Douglass's themes. He believed that the strength of the slave's resolve to resist slavery could be inferred from the necessity of oppression to keep her in chains. Were it not for resistance and fear of revolt, slaveholders would have no need for cruelty in maintaining order on the plantation. Though many whites argued that blacks were willing slaves, Douglass shattered the myth by indicating that the slaves possessed the same love of freedom as did whites, the same capacity to enjoy its fruits, and the same resolve to possess it. Douglass made this case for an audience on 14 October 1845:

> The slaveholders of America resort to every species of cruelty, but they can never reduce the slave to a willing obedience. The natural elasticity of the human soul repels the slightest attempt to enslave it. The black slaves of America are not wholly without that elasticity; they are men, and, being so, they do not submit readily to the yoke. It is easy to keep a brute in the position of a brute, but when you undertake to place a man in the same state,

believe me you must build your fences higher, and your doors firmer than before. A brute you may molest sometimes with impunity, but never a man.[22]

By appealing to the natural elasticity of the human soul, Douglass established his argument by that which united blacks and whites, the irreducible condition of being human that both shared equally. Douglass correctly perceived that proslavery hermeneutics denied the full humanity of blacks in order to sanction the enslavement of blacks. Douglass confronted his white audiences not only with their own racial biases but, moreover, with the humanity of slaves, a humanity that was stultified under the confines of chattel slavery. The relation between white prejudice and black subservience existed because of the power of whites to enforce their will and the powerlessness of blacks to reciprocate. The power dynamics of slavery were subsumed within discussions of black manhood and whites' denial of the humanity of their enslaved brothers and sisters.

God had given the negro a conscience and a will, but his conscience was no monitor to him, for he had no power to exercise his will, his master decided for him not only what he should eat and what he should drink, what he should wear, when and to whom he should speak, how much he should work, how much and by whom he is to be punished—he not only decided all these things, but what is morally right and wrong. The slave must not even choose his wife, must marry and unmarry at the will of this tyrant....[23]

The lack of power gave slaves the appearance of inferiority and lent legitimacy to false perceptions by whites.

---

[22] Douglass (14 October 1845), quoted in Blassingame, *The Frederick Douglass Papers*, 1:41.

[23] Douglass (10 November 1845), quoted in Blassingame, *The Frederick Douglass Papers*, 1:78.

Though he was confident of his logical rigor, Douglass knew that the perception of blacks by whites was predominant in the rationale for slavery. Douglass accounted for this reality by granting the condition of inferiority and attacking the logic behind slavery nonetheless. Douglass attacked the moral argument that blacks were rightly enslaved because of an inherent inferiority, before an audience at Cork, Ireland, in October 1845:

> What if we are inferior? Is it a valid reason for making slaves of us? For robbing us of our dearest rights? Can there be any reason found in moral or religious philosophy, justifying the enslaving of any class of beings, merely on the ground of their inferiority— intellectual, moral, or religious?...Notwithstanding our inferiority we have all the feelings common to humanity. I will grant frankly, I must grant, that the Negroes in America are inferior to the whites. But why are they so?...The people of America deprive us of every privilege—they turn round and taunt us with our inferiority! They stand upon our necks, they impudently taunt us, and ask the question, why we don't stand up erect? They tie our feet, and ask us why we don't run?...they turn round and ask, why we are not moral and intelligent; and tell us because we are not, that they have the right to enslave us.[24]

Douglass's concession of inferiority is somewhat misleading. He did not argue that the slave is any less human than the slave- holder. On the contrary, he asserted that both slave and master exhibit the same range of emotions, indicating the same degree of humanity. Slaves were not somehow less human than whites. They were, however, less powerful. And it is that powerlessness that caused them to be inferior in intellectual achievement. Conceding inferiority was merely conceding powerlessness. As a result, when

---

[24] Douglass (23 October 1845), quoted in Blassingame, *The Frederick Douglass Papers,* 1:60.

Douglass questioned whether inferiority was sufficient grounds for enslavement, he was actually asking whether the powerful possessed some moral or religious right to enslave the powerless. If lack of power was sufficient grounds for being enslaved, then many of his listeners in Ireland were in danger of being enslaved. If it could happen to blacks, it could happen to other powerless people. If being powerless was not a philosophically or morally compelling reason to justify one's enslavement, then it would be illogical and immoral to hold blacks in slavery unless some other compelling reason could be found.

Claims to a common humanity were at the core of another angle from which Douglass argued against slavery. Douglass believed in a great moral force, much like a seismic wave, that rolled across the world, picking up speed and washing away the dirt and decay of human sinfulness. This international reform impulse left the hope of healthier societies and a more just world in its wake. His emphasis on international reform indicates Douglass's indebtedness to the Garrisonian doctrines of universal reform and perfectionism. Swept up in the great reform impulse of the age, Douglass conveyed to audiences in America and in Europe his hope and expectation that moral reform would send slavery tottering to its grave. To this end, friends of abolition were also friends of temperance.

More than merely a spectator, Douglass participated in the spirit of international reform by pledging to become a teetotaler while in Dublin on 22 October 1845. He believed, moreover, that his act was not supererogatory, but a necessary component to the success of his antislavery work. Douglass expected that his behavior and temperance efforts were necessary to gain the emancipation of blacks in bondage and to guide freed blacks in the responsible use of their freedom. He confessed before a London audience that freedom and temperance were necessary to the well-being of blacks. "One great obstacle I have met with, has been the fact, that some of the colored people who have been redeemed from their chains, they have not made a good use of their freedom. I found, therefore, that in seeking to attain the object of my heart—the emancipation of my race from slavery—that I must also labor for the mental, moral, and religious elevation of those who had gained their freedom."[25] Freedom from slavery was a Pyrrhic victory at best if it was accompanied by mental, moral, and religious degeneration. Freedom, in the broadest sense of the term, embodied what Douglass referred to as "elevation" beyond emancipation. Emancipation without elevation was a hollow or incomplete freedom.

By foreswearing the use of "ardent spirits," one took the first step toward elevation and added energy to the reform impulse. In accordance with Douglass's convictions, even the temperance of his European audience would assist the emancipation and elevation of the slave. Douglass argued with great enthusiasm that public support for abolition was broadened by the spirit of temperance:

> I believe...that if we could but make the world sober, we would have no slavery. Mankind has been drunk. I believe that if the slaveholders would be sober for a moment—would consider the sinfulness of his position—hard-hearted as he is, I believe there is humanity enough if we could get him sober—we could get a public opinion sufficiently strong to break the relation of master and slave. All great reforms go together. Whatever tends to elevate, whatever tends to exalt humanity in one portion of the world, tends to exalt it in another part; the same feeling that warms the heart of the philanthropist here, animates that of the lover of humanity in every country.[26]

Douglass believed that Europeans would support emanci-pation in America because, in their zeal for reform, they actually supported the elevation of all humanity.

---

[25] Douglass (21 May 1846), quoted in Blassingame, *The Frederick Douglass Papers,* 1:266.

[26] Douglass, 23 October 1845, quoted in Blassingame, eds., *Frederick Douglass Papers,* 1:58.

Having tapped into the reform zeal of his European audience, Douglass hoped to infect his American audience with the same philanthropic urge. Garrison's gamble, the gamble of moral suasion, was made on such odds. For moral suasion to work, a critical mass of sympathizers was needed, who were willing to denounce American slavery in their newspapers and pulpits.

Douglass's international approach to ending slavery is correctly understood as an instance of Garrison's strategy of moral suasion. Americans were too mired in the politics of slavery to generate a moral force of the intensity that would prove necessary to defeat slavery. Outside assistance was required to build the requisite momentum. Douglass sought that assistance in England, Ireland, and Scotland:

> I have come here because slavery is such a gigantic system that one nation is not fit to cope with it—a system so deeply imbedded in the constitution of America, so firmly rooted in her churches, so entwined about the hearts of the whole people that it requires a moral force from without as well as within...America may boast of her abilities to build forts to stand the fire of the enemy, but she shall never be able to drive back that moral force which shall send slavery tottering to its grave.[27]

The international reform impulse upon which Douglass relied had its genesis in Western notions of natural rights and natural law. Conceptions of God-given rights and of the order found in nature drove Douglass's convictions that slavery upset the natural order and corrupted other civil institutions, thus calling for international reform to restore the natural balance.

In God's order, slaves have the same basic and inalienable rights enjoyed by all people. Chattel slavery abrogated those rights, in the process distorting God's order. God's order was restored through a process of moral rejuvenation.

---

[27] Douglass (17 March 1846), quoted in Blassingame, *The Frederick Douglass Papers*, 1:184.

First, God established that the slave is human. We know that God created the slave in God's image because God conceded rights to the slave. When questioned how the slave knew that he had rights, Douglass had a sure answer. "He knew he had rights, because he had powers. He had a right to think, because God had given him the power. He had a right to take care of his own person, because God had given him the power of doing so. Man had no right to take that power away, and the man who dared to do so, was a thief and a robber."[28] Douglass's argument here affirms that rights are indicated by the presence of powers or natural abilities. These abilities, an irreducible function of humanity, determine the extent to which people can claim rights. Individual and, presumably, corporate rights can be defended when as they do not trespass upon the powers of other moral agents. Douglass contended that slaves were human because they had a natural ability to think and to care for themselves. If slaves were human, then they had rights because God did not supply humans with natural abilities that they were unfit to exercise. To believe that slaves were even partially human compelled one to admit that slaves had, at the very least, some minimal rights. And if minimal rights were conceded, what right was more fundamental, more elementary to having a self than the right to think what one likes and to direct one's energies to freely chosen pursuits? Slavery, even in its mildest form, denied the most basic rights of human nature.

Beyond dehumanizing the slave, slavery also exerted a corrupting influence upon the civil and religious institutions of America. Douglass viewed this outcome as among the greatest evils of the "peculiar institution." One of slavery's greatest "and most potent evils was its corrupting influence not alone on the institutions of the society in which the bond-master moved, but also on all that came in contact with it, or even in its vicinity... it spread a dark cloud over the intellect of the nation, corrupting the channels of morality, poisoning the fountains of religion and

---

[28] Douglass (15 January 1846), quoted in Blassingame, *The Frederick Douglass Papers*, 1:137.

perverting the beneficial objects of government."[29] Perverse to its core, slavery impeded the proper functioning of government. It even vitiated the traditional conduits of moral instruction, conduits that kept government on the right track. As a result, the nation lacked the ability to right itself through the usual legal channels. Civil law was irreparably corrupted by the influence of slavery.

Finally, given that civil institutions were corrupted beyond repair, the demise of slavery had to come about through atonement or moral rejuvenation. Moral suasion was the only means able to effect the kind of rejuvenation needed. Further, for moral suasion to remain undefiled, union with slaveholders had to be abolished.

THE RELIGIOUS AGENDA

In order for moral suasion to be successful, Garrison understood that it must rely heavily upon an interpretation of scripture that reinforced the central thrust of his position. His movement was a Christian one, and as such, his principles had to be compatible with the Bible.

Douglass is not remembered for being a religious thinker, and it is difficult to know the extent to which he would have relied upon scripture were it not for Garrison's influence. As it stands, Douglass referred to better than seventy Biblical passages in speeches during his tenure with the Garrisonians. Most of these references are devoid of any considerable exegetical content. Yet they are not merely passing references. Douglass showed signs of referring to the same scripture over time when narrating a particular event or asserting a particular argument. He clearly gave some thought to effective uses of scripture, and repeated those verses that he felt most compelling.

On occasion, Douglass contrasted Biblical passages in order to compare proslavery and abolitionist hermeneutics. In some speeches, Douglass referred to as many as five or six Biblical

---

[29] Douglass (17 October 1845), quoted in Blassingame, *The Frederick Douglass Papers*, 1:46.

texts. In these cases, his use of scripture was much like his use of narrative in that it served to reinforce a moral argument.

Douglass relied largely on New Testament texts, but he also made considerable reference to the Old Testament. He relied upon Torah, Wisdom Literature, and the Prophets to shame his opposition into contrition. By the early 1850s, when Douglass broke from Garrison's camp, his reference to scripture changed as well. Old Testament fire and brimstone became more commonplace for Douglass, replacing, to some extent, the more forgiving New Testament injunctions that pervaded his earlier addresses.

Douglass used scripture in three distinct ways. First, he used scripture to challenge proslavery hermeneutics. He laid bare the inconsistencies and fallacies that undermined the scriptural interpretation favored by the advocates of slavery. Second, Douglass employed scripture to assert what he deemed to be true religion. More than merely asserting the deficiencies of the proslavery case, Douglass offered his account of what the nation would be like freed from its reliance upon a religion that justified slavery and that promoted inequality. Third, Douglass invoked scripture to defend his moral arguments. This was his most common appeal to the Bible. By quoting scripture as an authoritative source to endorse his moral agenda, Douglass legitimized the agenda and challenged the proslavery case.

Douglass believed that the proslavery case was founded largely on three scriptural warrants: Ephesians 6:5-8; Luke 12:47; and, Genesis 9:18–27. The New Testament passages affirm that slavery is compatible with Christian practice. The Old Testament passage, referred to as the Curse of Ham, explains why sub-Saharan Africans were enslaved over against any other race of people.

Ephesians 6:5–8, as taken from the RSV,[30] renders: "Slaves, be obedient to those who are your earthly masters, with fear and trembling, in singleness of heart, as to Christ, not in the way of eye service, as men-pleasers, but as servants of Christ, doing the will of God from the heart, rendering service with a good will as to the

---

[30] I refer to the Revised Standard Version of the Bible when citing the texts.

Lord and not to men, knowing that whatever good any one does, he will receive the same again from the Lord, whether he is a slave or free." This prescript is found also in Colossians 3:22 and in Titus 2:9, which adds the themes of submissiveness and fidelity as well. According to the advocates of slavery, God intended slavery, sanctioned slavery, and expected slaves to perform willingly.

Disobedient slaves could expect the lash. Contrary to Douglass's assertion that the lash symbolized the moral turpitude of slavery, proslavery advocates argued that the lash was a part of God's plan. They referenced Luke 12:47 in their defense: "and that servant who knew his master's will, but did not make ready or act according to his will, shall receive a severe beating." Douglass remarked on numerous occasions that this passage was the favorite one cited to slaves during religious services in the South. He noted this passage more than any other.

Those who defended the divine sanction of American slavery argued that God intended Africans, and only Africans, to be slaves. Biblical exegetes cited Noah's curse on his son, Ham, in Genesis 9:24–27 as a justification for the enslavement of Africans: "When Noah awoke from his wine and knew what his youngest son had done to him, he said, "cursed be Canaan; a slave of slaves shall he be to his brothers." He also said, "Blessed by the Lord my God be Shem; and let Canaan be his slave. God enlarge Japeth, and let him dwell in the tents of Shem; and let Canaan be his slave."

The matter of the curse was hotly contested. In his work entitled, *Bible Defence of Slavery*, Josiah Priest wrote a common interpretation of the passage. He argued that Noah's three sons represented three distinct races. He determined that Japeth was a "blue eyed white man."[31] Further, wrote Priest, Noah's racial characteristics had been passed on to Japheth "on whose face and form was stamped in the eye of his father, the sure sign of great intellectual endowments betokening renown, enlargement and rule

---

[31] Josiah Priest, *Bible Defense of Slavery* (Louisville KY: Willis A. Bush, 1851) 79.

among men..."[32] Shem, the red or copper colored son, was the genealogical father of the patriarchs, the prophets, the Jews, and of Jesus Christ. Ham is cited by Priest as "a wooly headed, black eyed, black man."[33] Priest depicts Ham in great detail:

> But, in addition to what is already said representing the Hebrew word "Ham," we may remark that it was, in some sense, also prophetic of Ham's character and fortunes in his own life, and the fortunes of his race, as the word not only signified black in its literal sense, but pointed out the very disposition of his mind. The word, doubtless, has more meanings than we are now acquainted with—two of which, however, beside the first, we find are heat or violence of temper, exceedingly prone to acts of ferocity and cruelty, involving murder, war, butcheries, and even cannibalism, including beastly lusts, and lasciviousness in its worst feature, going beyond the force of these passions, as possessed in common by the other races of men. Second, the word signifies deceit, dishonesty, treachery, low-mindedness, and malice. What a group of horrors are here, couched in the word Ham, all agreeing, in a most surprising manner, with the color of Ham's skin, as well as with his real character as a man, during his own life, as well as with that of his race, even now.[34]

Priest concluded that "it is not sinful to enslave the negro race, providing it is done in a tender, fatherly and thoughtful manner...."[35]

Abolitionists railed against such arguments. Presbyterian minister John Rankin, for example, took issue with several points raised in the proslavery argument from the Curse of Ham. First, Rankin argued that the curse fell on Canaan, one of Ham's sons,

---

[32] Ibid., 43.
[33] Ibid., 79.
[34] Ibid., 40.
[35] Ibid., 41.

and not on Ham. Rankin contended further that the curse did not extend to the rest of Ham's sons:

> The rest of Ham's sons it seems were innocent, and consequently were not included in it. The history of the world shows that many of the nations which descended from them have been respectable, and subjected to no calamities but such are common to the rest of mankind. Hence it is as plain as stubborn fact can make it, that the curse did not include all of Ham's posterity. It was denounced against Canaan and history shows that it fell upon his posterity. Our Africans did not descend from him, and therefore were not with him consigned to servitude.[36]

Second, Rankin maintained that the "doom was not perpetual," and that the curse was fulfilled when the Israelites conquered the Canaanites.[37] Since that time, Rankin argued, "the Canaanites have mingled with other nations, and so do not now exist as a distinct people, and consequently the term of their servitude must be terminated."[38]

Douglass, too, railed against the argument that Africans were the scriptural descendants of Ham and, therefore, deserved to be enslaved. He countered the argument by appealing to the rape of black women at the hands of white men and to the rise of biracial slaves. "If the lineal descendants of Ham are alone to be scripturally enslaved, it is certain that slavery at the South must soon become unscriptural; for thousands are ushered into the world, annually, who, like myself, owe their existence to white fathers, and those fathers most frequently their own masters."[39]

---

[36] John Rankin, quoted in William Pease and Jane Pease, eds., *The Antislavery Argument,* (New York: The Bobbs-Merrill Company, Inc., 1965) 119.

[37] Ibid.

[38] Ibid., 120.

[39] Frederick Douglass, *Narrative of the Life of Frederick Douglass, An American Slave, Written by Himself* (Boston: 1845), in Henry Louis Gates, Jr.,

Douglass did not concede to the proslavery interpretation of scripture. Rather, he argued extensively from six texts that challenged the three primary proslavery texts. These passages are: Genesis 1:26; Exodus 20:15; Leviticus 19:18 (and Matthew 7:12); Deuteronomy 23:15; and, Philemon 15–16.

The first of the passages considered, Genesis 1:26, enabled Douglass to assert the humanity of the slaves. The text reads, "Then God said, 'Let us make man in our image, after our likeness....' " Douglass used the text to challenge the argument that God intended for humans, created in the very likeness of God, to be enslaved. Even when the proslavery camp countered with other passages from scripture, Douglass pushed them to acknowledge the fundamental humanity of slaves and the likeness of God irreducibly embedded in that humanity. The ideologues of the "peculiar institution" were unable to counter the argument that slaves were human. The best they could hope to argue was the inferiority of the slave, for her imperfect humanity. As a result, they could not claim definitively that slaves were not created in the image of God. To admit even partial humanity, allowed for the possibility of even partial God-likeness. Texts such as Genesis 1:26 helped to push the religious debate into another arena, away from questions of the humanity of slaves, and toward questions of the legitimacy of slavery in light of the slaves attested humanity.

Douglass's description of the whipping of "Old Barney," makes the point. Although he did not refer to Genesis 1:26 directly, Douglass argued the equal humanity of blacks and whites:

> One of the most heart-saddening and humiliating scenes I ever witnessed, was the whipping of Old Barney, by Col. Lloyd himself. Here were two men, both advanced in years; there were the silvery locks of Col. L., and there was the bald and toil-worn brow of Old Barney; master and slave; superior and inferior here, but equals at

---

ed. *Frederick Douglass/Autobiographies* (New York: Library of America/Penguin Books, 1994) 17–18.

the bar of God; and in the common course of events, they must both soon meet in another world, in a world where all distinctions, except those based on obedience and disobedience, are blotted out forever.[40]

Building upon his conception of the *imago Dei*, Douglass referred to the Hebrew scripture's Decalogue to condemn the practice of slavery. Exodus 20:15 condemns theft. Douglass used this verse to appraise slavery as theft, and slaveholders as thieves. The verse countered arguments of the morality of legal slave transactions, based upon Ephesians 6:5, by appealing to a preemptive divine command. Douglass argued from the verse to rebut claims that slavery was morally permissible. Slavery was theft, and unlike the theft of an animal, it entailed the theft of one created in God's image. In the appendix to his 1845 narrative, Douglass took up the issue of theft:

We have men-stealers for ministers, women-whippers for missionaries, and cradle-plun-derers for church mem-bers. The man who wields the blood-clotted cowskin dur-ing the week fills the pulpit on Sunday, and claims to be a minister of the meek and lowly Jesus. The man who robs me of my earnings at the end of each week meets me as a class-leader on Sunday morning, to show me the way of life, and the path of salvation...we see the thief preaching against theft.[41]

Douglass was not alone in his reliance on passages from Genesis and Exodus to make his argument. The Garrisonians also held that slaves were created in the image of God and that slavery was theft. Consider an excerpt from the writings of Stephen S. Foster, of whom Douglass wrote, "No white man ever made the

---

[40] Douglass, *My Bondage and My Freedom*, 194.
[41] Douglass, *Narrative of the Life of Frederick Douglass*, 97–98.

black man's cause more completely his own."[42] According to Foster, "To steal is to take that which belongs to another without his consent. Theft and robbery are, morally, the same act, differing only in form. Both are included under the command, "thou shalt not steal"—that is, thou shalt not take thy neighbor's property... no proposition is plainer than that every man owns his own industry... every slaveholder takes the entire industry of his slaves... no matter how kind or humane the master may be, he lives by plunder."[43]

The vulnerability of slaves to the financial interests of their owners often made marriage between slaves an temporary union, devoid of the sacramental meaning and significance intended by scripture. Douglass cited Exodus 20:14, "You shall not commit adultery," in order to identify one of the more pernicious consequences of slavery. Slaveholders made adulterers of slaves by refusing to let slaves marry according to Christian rites and customs. Without the benefit of Christian marriage, or of divorce, without the ability to defend one's family from separation by the sale of family members, without the power to prevent rape at the hands of the slaveowner—slaves had little incentive to form monogamous, committed unions. On the contrary, slaveholders often encouraged slaves to indulge in sexual relations without responsibility. Douglass applied Exodus 14 not to castigate slaves but to chastise slaveholders for what they forced slaves to do.

The scripture verse also was used to condemn directly the sexually abusive acts of slaveholders. In one particularly pointed passage, Foster reasoned that slaveholders were little more than rapists:

By converting woman into a commodity, to be bought and sold and used by her claimant as his avarice or lust may dictate, he totally annihilates the marriage

---

[42] Frederick Douglass, *Life and Times of Frederick Douglass* (Hartford CT, 1881), in Henry Louis Gates, Jr., ed. *Frederick Douglass/Autobiographies* (New York: Library of America/Penguin Books, 1994) 667.

[43] Stephen S. Foster, quoted in Pease and Pease, *The Antislavery Argument*, 135.

institution; and transforms the wife into what he very significantly terms a "breeder," and her children as "stock." This change in a woman's condition from a free moral agent to a chattel, places her domestic relations entirely beyond her own control, and makes her a mere instrument for the gratification of another's desires.[44]

Foster concluded the line of thought by condemning slaveholders as rapists who deserved to die for their crimes.

Leviticus 19:18 and Matthew 7:12 establish the ethical injunction to neighbor-love, an injunction which finds its foremost expression in the "second commandment" found in Mark 12:31. Slavery violated God's law in part because it transgressed God's command to love one's neighbor as oneself. Even though Leviticus 19:17–18 applies the neighbor-love provision to fellow Israelites, verses 33–34 extend the provision to include sojourners.

Matthew 7:12 explains the meaning of neighbor-love: "So whatever you wish that men would do to you, do so to them; for this is the law and the prophets." Taken in conjunction with Leviticus 19:18, the verses enabled Douglass to insist that even if one did not think of the slave as a neighbor, the neighbor-love injunction still applied by virtue of what is commonly called the Golden Rule. This line of argument was popular among the Garrisonians.

Garrison argued extensively from the Golden Rule. He employed it in contrast to what he called the "proslavery interpretations of a time-serving clergy," with "the standard of eternal justice."[45] The Golden Rule supplied the standard of justice, but the "rights of man," in Garrison's words, were derived "from his own nature" and not "from any book."[46]

Douglass was not deaf to those advocates of slavery who maintained that the relationship between master and slave was exempt from the neighbor-love command. He quoted Deuter-

---

[44] Ibid., 137–38.

[45] William Lloyd Garrison, quoted in Pease and Pease, *The Antislavery Argument*, 131.

[46] Ibid., 132.

onomy 23:15 in order to establish that runaway slaves ought not be returned to their masters: "You shall not give up to his master a slave who has escaped from his master to you." Verse 16 follows, "he shall dwell with you, in your midst, in the place which he shall choose within one of your towns, where it pleases him best; you shall not oppress him." Douglass believed that slavery could not continue to exist without the assistance of the North, primarily in returning fugitive slaves to their owners in the South. For Douglass, one did not have to think of the slave as a neighbor to be obligated by the injunction set forth in Deuteronomy 23:15.

Douglass also cited Philemon 15–16 to bolster the argument that Christians in the North ought not participate in the return of fugitive slaves to the South. The verses describe the return of the fugitive slave Onesimus to Philemon "no longer as a slave but more than a slave, as a beloved brother."[47] Fugitive slaves, or, more specifically, those fugitive slaves who confess Jesus as Christ, should not be returned because they would not be welcomed as brothers but punished as criminals.

Douglass threw down the gauntlet before his proslavery opponents and challenged them to defend not only the rationale for slavery, but also to defend American slavery as an ontological expression of God's kingdom. The case for slavery, as Douglass understood it, failed to trump the case against slavery. He believed that his case countered the proslavery platform. But, lest his audiences should believe that slavery was simply an intractable moral issue, Douglass quoted scripture to portray his view of true Christianity as opposed to the sham Christianity supported by the opponents of abolition and emancipation. He interpreted what he deemed to be the tone and tenor of Christianity, its spirit, and he argued that his interpretation of scripture was more in keeping with that spirit than was the case advocated by proslavers.

The argument for "true religion," as he called it, marked a second major use of scripture for Douglass. By referring to scripture in this manner, Douglass disallowed even the possibility that the proslavery case was consistent with scripture. On the contrary,

---

[47] Philem. 15–16.

Douglass treated the proslavery case as an exemplification of false Christianity.

In one of his oft-repeated tracts on true Christian practice, Douglass contrasted the two versions of Christianity:

> I love the religion of our blessed Savior. I love that religion that comes from above, in the "wisdom of God, which is first pure, then peaceable, gentle, and easy to be entreated, full of mercy and good fruits, without partiality and without hypocrisy"[JAS 3:17]. I love that religion that sends its votaries to bind up the wounds of him that has fallen among thieves. I love that religion that makes it the duty of its disciples to visit the fatherless and the widow in their affliction. I love that religion that is based upon the glorious principle of love to God and love to man; which makes its followers do unto others as they themselves would be done by....It is because I love this religion that I hate the woman-whipping, the mind-darkening, the soul-destroying religion that exists in the southern [sic] states of America. It is because I regard the one as good, and pure, and holy, that I cannot but regard the other as bad, corrupt, and wicked. Loving the one I must hate the other; holding to the one I must reject the other.[48]

Douglass invoked James 3:17 to distinguish true religion from the apostasy of Southern religion. He reasoned that one who accepted that text as truth would be hard-pressed to demonstrate how the religion of the Southern states embodied its plain sense. On the contrary, Douglass argued that one who paid more than lip service to the verse would be compelled to see the reasonableness of his case. Slavery was simply incongruous with God's will as established in the first, seventh, and eighth commandments of the Decalogue, in the Golden Rule injunction of Matthew 7:12, and in

---

[48] Douglass (12 May 1846), quoted in Foner, *The Life and Writings of Frederick Douglass*, 1:162.

the commandment to love one's neighbor as oneself. Further, slavery was incompatible with the gist of God's Word as described in James 3:17.

At this point in his career, Douglass was willing to reason with the advocates of slavery, interpreting scripture to defend his moral agenda. In subsequent years, however, he spent less time reasoning and interpreting scripture and more time prophesying against those who maintained the system of slavery.

As he neared his break with Garrison, his tone grew more stern and his message more focused. Speaking before an audience in his adopted hometown of Rochester, New York, in December 1850, Douglass argued that slavery made gods of slaveholders:

> Slavery is a sin, in that it comprehends a monstrous violation of the great principle of human liberty, to which I have endeavored thus to draw your attention. In this respect, it is a direct war upon the government of God. In subjecting one man to the arbitrary control of another, it contravenes the first command of the Decalogue; and as upon that command rests the whole superstructure of justice, purity and brotherly kindness, slavery may be justly regarded as a warfare against all the principles of infinite goodness.[49]

True religion did not tolerate woman-whipping, nor did it violate the first command of the Decalogue, "Thou shalt have no other gods before me."[50] Slavery made slaveholders god-like in the power they exercised over slaves. Further, it denied slaves liberty to worship God. According to this interpretation, subjecting one moral agent to the arbitrary control of another contravened the God-first command insofar as it deified one party and disallowed the other from putting God first.

---

[49] Douglass (8 December 1850), quoted in Blassingame, eds., *The Frederick Douglass Papers*, 2:262.

[50] Exod. 20:3 RSV.

Douglass also appealed to religion to underscore his moral arguments. He believed that too many Christians, especially slaveholding Christians, simply lost sight of the moral life. Their preoccupation with the Word of God induced moral myopia. God, and not neighbor, became their focal point. As Douglass's argued the point, "The great difficulty about our Christianity is, we have got certain notions about religion that turn off our attention from humanity altogether. We think that religion is the entertainment of a hope."[51]

Douglass lamented the decline of "true religion" as he described it:

> I believe the grand reason why we have slavery in this land at the present moment is that we are too religious as a nation, in other words, that we have substituted religion for humanity—we have substituted a form of Godliness, an outside show for the real thing itself. We have houses built for the worship of God, which we regard as too sacred to plead the cause of the down-trodden millions in them. They will tell you in these churches that they are willing to receive you to talk to them about the sins of the scribes and the Pharisees, or on the subject of the heathenism of the South Sea Islanders...but the very minute you ask them to open their mouths for the liberation of the southern [sic] slaves, they tell you, that is a subject with which they have nothing to do, and which they do not wish to have introduced into the church; it is foreign to the object for which churches in this country were formed, and houses built.[52]

Douglass feared that God was becoming dispensable to religion, replaced by an odd assemblage of Bible verses, cultural

---

[51] Douglass (9 May 1849), quoted in Blassingame, *The Frederick Douglass Papers*, 2:189.

[52] Ibid., 2:180.

mores, and economic interests that had little to do with God's kingdom.

This type of quote has come to characterize Douglass on religion. Taken out of context, it suggests a man who harbored a great deal of hostility toward religion. It is closer to the truth to see in his words a growing frustration with the hypocrisy, self-centeredness, and flagrant immorality practiced by those who were the custodians of moral probity. They perverted the Gospel and cloaked their immorality in its verses. For his part, Douglass was neither anti-religious nor irreligious. He was discontented with what he believed to be an other-worldly religion that lent itself to sanctimonious pronouncements but was deaf to cries for justice and blind to its own culpability.

Interestingly, his invective fell as heavily upon the black church as upon the white church. Black clergy and white were blamed for the perpetuation of slavery. In the case of black clergy, Douglass held them responsible for failing to promote a message of self-help. "The clergy are to blame for the apathy of the colored people to their own cause. The text, 'Seek ye first the kingdom of heaven, and its righteousness,' etc., has been grossly perverted by the ignorant colored clergy, so that the people wait for God to help them. It is a ridiculous and absurd notion to expect God to deliver us from bondage. We must elevate ourselves by our own efforts."[53]

Douglass did not argue that there is no God. Rather, his message was closer to the conviction that God helps those who help themselves. The message of self-help is one of several marking Douglass's departure from the Garrisonians and indicating his mature thought as a political abolitionist and editor of the *North Star*. Along with the message of self-help to blacks, Douglass railed against advocates of African re-colonization, while championing integration and equal rights for blacks in America.

In addition to these shifts of emphases in his moral agenda, Douglass's use of the Bible changed as well. Douglass relied

---

[53] Douglass (7 May 1849), ibid., 2:170.

increasingly on verses such as Genesis 42:21, Isaiah 48:22, and Revelation 13:10 to condemn directly the practitioners of slavery.[54] Whereas his moral case against slavery expanded as he matured to encompass the new moral themes noted above, his religious case against slavery diminished. With the passing of time, Douglass showed less tolerance for religious debate and relied on scripture to shame and condemn his opponents rather than to persuade them. Two verses he cited to achieve that end were Revelation 21:1 and 21:27. The former speaks of a new heaven and a new earth after the first earth passes away. Revelation 21:27 adds: "But nothing unclean shall enter it, nor any one who practices abomination or falsehood, but only those who are written in the Lamb's book of life." Douglass sent a chilling message to advocates of slavery that they stood in eternal peril. Beyond asserting true religion, Douglass devoted more attention to the character of the practitioners of slavery and not merely the institution of slavery. He began to prophesy about the shape of things to come.

CONCLUSION

This chapter began with the question, What was Garrison's influence on Douglass's moral and religious thought? To answer, one must remember that Douglass's introduction to abolitionist thought occurred prior to his introduction to Garrison's version of it. According to his autobiographical accounts, he became conscious of the term "abolition" and its meaning during his years in Baltimore. Douglass was approximately twelve years old, by his own calculation, when he got hold of a copy of the *Columbian Orator*. The book, and a city newspaper called the *Baltimore*

---

[54] "There is no peace for the wicked" (Isa. 48.22 RSV); "Then they said to one another, 'In truth we are guilty concerning our brother, in that we saw the distress of his soul, when he besought us and we would not listen; therefore is this distress come upon us'" (Gen. 42.21 RSV); "If any one is to be taken captive, to captivity he goes; if any one slays with the sword must he be slain. Here is a call for the endurance and faith of the saints" (Rev. 13.10 RSV).

American, were the first vehicles that introduced Douglass to abolitionist thought. It would be at least eight years before he became familiar with Garrison's own writings through the *Liberator*.

Douglass suggested in his final autobiographical account that he became a Garrisonian by chance, simply because he was introduced to Garrison and to his brand of abolitionist thought.

> Brought directly, when I escaped from slavery, into contact with abolitionists who regarded the Constitution as a slaveholding instrument, and finding their views supported by the united and entire history of every department of the government, it is not strange that I assumed the Constitution to be just what these friends made it seem to be. I was bound, not only by their superior knowledge, to take their opinions in respect to this subject, as the true ones, but also because I had no means of showing the unsoundness of these opinions. But for the responsibility of conducting a public journal, and the necessity imposed upon me of meeting opposite views from abolitionists outside of New England, I should in all probability have remained firm in my disunion views.[55]

The logic of the case for maintaining the union was compelling. Essentially, disunion could disrupt Southern slavery by breaching the comity between North and South, but it was no guarantor of emancipation. If runaway slaves were not returned to the South, if they could rely on the promise of freedom in the North, then perhaps they themselves would strike the greatest blow against their servitude by fleeing the South in larger numbers. On the other hand, disunion, if successful, would mean that those slaves trapped in the South would be all but forgotten. If the union were dissolved, slavery would still continue in the South, even while the Garrisonians celebrated their victory. What then would be the fate of those slaves remaining in the South?

---

[55] Douglass, *Life and Times of Frederick Douglass*, 705.

Maintaining the union offered, at the very least, the promise of ending slavery and not merely localizing it. No slave would be left behind. For one committed to the emancipation of his people, unionism provided Douglass with an assurance of ongoing attention to the plight of all slaves. Once he conceded the persuasiveness of the arguments for union, Douglass embarked upon what some scholars have described as a philosophical turning point. That is to say, he openly declared that he no longer viewed the Constitution as a proslavery document. As a corollary to this new understanding for the need for union, Douglass affirmed the Constitution as a guarantor of equality and of civil rights. Further, he endorsed political action over moral suasion, and in rejecting the last major tenet of Garrisonian abolition, supported voting as a necessary tool of political action. By May 1851 the change was complete.

Douglass broke with Garrison not because of a philosophical disagreement but due to his greater clarity about the effectiveness of various strategies to emancipate and elevate black people. Philosophically, Douglass was still committed to the same basic ends. A change in the means employed to satisfy those ends reflects more a pragmatic reassessment than a philosophical rupture. Garrison's view of the Constitution was not wrong by interpretive error as much as it was dangerous to the ends of emancipation; it was a strategic error.

Douglass had enough familiarity with both sides of the argument to appreciate the strengths and weaknesses of both positions. He argued that the Constitution was a proslavery document in a debate in Syracuse on 17 January 1850. In that debate he engaged his opponents by arguing that unionism was a pretense to uphold something that did not exist. The slaveholders, Douglass argued, knew of "no such union" as professed by the Liberty Party.[56] In defending disunion, Douglass was defending honesty in dealing with deceitful slaveholders. The Liberty Party

---

[56] Douglass (17 January 1850), quoted in Blassingame, *The Frederick Douglass Papers*, 2:221.

also advocated disunion, Douglass continued, "but in a covert way, without declaring that to be the object."[57]

Although Douglass changed his position on the status of the Constitution, he did not alter the supporting beliefs that lead him to such a position. He did not suddenly come to believe that the union professed by the Liberty Party really did exist. Nor did he believe that slaveholders would adopt the Liberty Party's view of the union. There were no discernible changes in his pragmatic convictions to warrant the idea that his altered view on the Constitution derived from philosophic conversion. In sum, Douglass decided upon an alternate strategy that was more consistent with his mature moral and religious thought. Douglass's growing emphasis on moral themes such as self-help, integration, equality, human rights, and civil rights fit neatly within the Liberty Party's emphasis on political action.

The break with Garrison became necessary because Douglass came to realize that political action, with its emphasis on self-motivation and self-reliance, suited him better than did moral suasion's emphasis on God's Word. Both methods relied on winning over the uncommitted masses, but moral suasion, in the absence of political action, encouraged political powerlessness and an over-dependence on divine intervention to accomplish social reform. Douglass viewed this mix as dangerous to the cause.

What then, finally, is one to make of the Garrisonian episode in the life of Douglass? The question can be answered in several ways. In general, the Garrisonian episode provided Douglass with national and international exposure, name recognition, greater familiarity with proslavery and antislavery arguments, and experience in public speaking. These factors proved essential to Douglass's maturation as an abolitionist. Further, Garrison proved to be a moral exemplar whose views established a benchmark for Douglass.

The Garrisonian episode accomplished even more than these. Much like the time he spent in Baltimore, the time spent with the

---

[57] Ibid.

Garrisonians provided Douglass with an opportunity to sharpen his cognitive tools, an incentive to pursue his ambition, and hope that his skill and ambition would well prepare him to do great work.

4

THE DOUGLASS EPISODE

> Surely, the Frederick Douglass of 1853, is a very different
> man from the one of 1846.... He is an altered man in his
> temper and spirit.[1]

The Garrisonians were on to something. Though Douglass disagreed with their assessment of him as egotistical and ungenerous, he nonetheless reprinted an article from the *Liberator*, "Frederick Douglass and His Paper." By 1853 Douglass was indeed a changed man, far different than during his days as an agent of the Massachusetts Anti-Slavery Society. Douglass himself was the first to acknowledge that change. If the younger Douglass was ever pressed to hold his tongue, the editor of the *North Star* was free of any such obligations and wielded his pen with the abandon of a man who would neither be silenced nor constrained.

From 1851, when he broke from Garrison's formidable camp, until the dawn of the Civil War, Douglass experienced a period of great energy and pronounced intellectual activity. Reflecting on those days in his 1893 memoirs, he wrote, "if I have at any time said or written that which is worth remembering or repeating, I

---

[1] *Frederick Douglass' Paper* (Rochester NY), 9 December 1853. Reprint of "Frederick Douglass and His Paper," first published in the *Liberator*.

must have said such things between the years 1848 and 1860."[2] For students of Douglass the period is indeed rich in yield. Douglass's tenure as editor of the *North Star* and *Frederick Douglass' Paper* mark the years of his maturity as a thinker.

This chapter examines Douglass's moral thought around the time of his departure from the Garrisonians, and his political thought shortly after that as a convert to the Liberty Party. Douglass's political thought exerted controlling influence on his moral and religious thought. A pragmatic reassessment of the means employed to achieve his goals led Douglass from an emphasis on moral suasion alone to a mix of moral suasion and political action. Douglass did not abandon moral suasion as a strategy, but Garrison's idea that the two were incompatible. The suasionist strategy resisted political compromise with slave holders. Moral suasion held motivational significance for many abolitionists in that it provided both a reliable moral compass and a fixed destination, but it provided little of the tactical direction that Douglass desired. Moral suasion also failed to lay plans for the elevation of blacks after emancipation. Finally, by endorsing disunion it conceded the continuation of slavery in the South. For its part, disunionism, although tactical, led the movement in the wrong socioeconomic direction. Douglass increasingly turned to political action as the avenue through which to accomplish the messy work of emancipation and elevation. Where once he cast the problem of slavery exclusively in moral terms, Douglass began to cast the problem primarily in political terms. Though he did not entirely jettison the moral case against slavery, he increasingly referred to it from a political frame of reference.

The politicization of thought is one index of Douglass's maturity. This later thought reflects a mix of elements including: rejection of certain features of Garrisonian doctrine; indebtedness to the political philosophy of Gerrit Smith and the Liberty Party;

---

[2] Frederick Douglass, *Life and Times of Frederick Douglass* (Hartford CT: 1881), in Henry Louis Gates, Jr., ed. *Frederick Douglass/Autobiographies* (New York: Library of America/Penquin Books, 1994), 709.

heightened race-consciousness; and, exposure to philosophers and essayists of his day.

Maturity in the case of Douglass does not mean "original thought" as much as it means "worked out fully by the mind." As an advocate of the Liberty Party, Douglass resolved his misgivings about Garrisonian abolitionism. He adopted instead a more flexible system that responded to the political events of the day, maintained its goal of universal and immediate emancipation, and provided a means of structuring elevation after emancipation.

To be sure, there are moments of originality in Douglass's thought. In June 1854, for example, Douglass explained a feature of his moral philosophy in an editorial entitled, "Is it Right and Wise to Kill a Kidnapper?"[3] It is one of the few formal, sustained arguments in the Douglass corpus, one that he himself referred to as original. The piece appeared at the time when the Liberty Party had entered into its death throes as an organization. It displays Douglass's increasingly independent moral thought as it related to either Garrison or Smith.

Douglass's ability to discern the nuances between the white and black abolitionist agenda, and his increased willingness to align himself with the latter further marks his mature thought. This change indicates that Douglass settled into a new niche in the abolitionist cause. While he maintained close connection to white abolitionists, he saw clearly the limits of their ability to elevate blacks. Even sympathetic whites struggled with institutionalized racism. They could not effect elevation for blacks. Whites could assist, but the primary work of it belonged to blacks. Douglass adapted his role as moral exemplar to shoulder this burden and help create change from within the black community. More than merely symbolizing for whites the character and achievement of black people, Douglass prescribed for blacks a way to make entry into middle-class society. Achieving this objective in light of institutionalized racism would require blacks to attain a degree of social cohesion, or at least generalized agreements about how to

---

[3] Frederick Douglass, "Is it Right and Wise to Kill A Kidnapper?" *Frederick Douglass' Paper* (Rochester NY), 2 June 1854.

proceed in that direction. Douglass hoped to guide this conversation. Douglass became more of a black nationalist in his writings.[4] On one occasion, Douglass criticized a black abolitionist who proposed to speak not as a black man but as a man. Douglass countered that he could make no such distinction for himself. This heightened race-consciousness influenced his ethics. In addition to the moral issues that he addressed previously, his editorials are dotted with tracts specifically for blacks on practical equality, character, self-reliance, resistance, and on white assumptions of black inferiority, all of which were beyond the scope of white abolitionists.

Though the subject matter of Douglass's editorials corresponded to that of his lectures, they disclosed a side of his thinking that was less structured, less constrained by the philosophy of party and that ranged more freely over the moral and political landscape.

Moreover, unlike his lectures which were tailored to specific audiences, the editorials were written largely for free blacks, and intended to inspire them to succeed as a people. Douglass enjoyed a familiarity in them with fellow blacks that was not possible in large lecture halls before white audiences. Unfortunately for Douglass, few subscribers were black. Most of his subscribers and readers, presumably, were white. Yet that did not prevent Douglass from writing tracts for a black audience. In an editorial from 1848 Douglass defended self-reliance as an index of character:

> If there be one evil spirit among us... it is that lazy, mean and cowardly spirit, that robs us of all manly self-reliance, and teaches us to depend upon others for the accomplishment of that which we should achieve with our own hands. Our white friends can and are rapidly

---

[4] Douglass remained an integrationist even as he championed black "nationalism." Here the term does not indicate social, political, or economic separation from whites. By "nationalism" Douglass had in mind a common consciousness among blacks in view of institutionalized racism, and a strategy necessary to achieve broad social integration.

removing the barriers to our improvement, which [they] themselves have set up; but the main work must be commenced, carried on, and concluded by ourselves.... It is evident that we can be improved and elevated only just so fast and far as we shall improve and elevate ourselves. We must rise or fall, succeed or fail, by our own merits. For our part, we despise a freedom and equality obtained for us by others, and for which we have been unwilling to labor....What we, the colored people want is character, and this nobody can give us.[5]

Though self-reliance was not a novel theme to Douglass in 1848, the tone of the editorial suggests the writer was not merely a race-neutral abolitionist but a black abolitionist. White abolitionists could fight for the demise of slavery, but they could not ensure that freedom would effect the desired socio-economic improvement in the black community. Douglass understood that black abolitionists had a particular responsibility to cultivate a spirit of achievement within a people who had little opportunity for success. In his editorials he [sought/hoped/endeavored to]inspire readers, not as a Garrisonian abolitionist, but as one within their ranks. he emphasized his own experience as a black man, one who suffered their oppression and dreamed their dreams, demonstrating all the while that blacks were capable of success, even when competing with whites.

Douglass's evolution from Garrisonian abolitionism to black activism foreshadowed the change in his political platform. Prior to his conversion on the issue of the constitutionality of slavery, Douglass recognized that the effective black abolitionists, in virtue of what I am calling their *particular responsibility*, had to concern themselves with the elevation of the black community following emancipation. Moral suasion, perhaps a strategy for promoting emancipation, was not suited to the work that remained to be done following emancipation. Post-emancipation efforts would neces-

---

[5] Frederick Douglass, "What are the Colored People doing for Themselves?" *North Star* (Rochester NY), 14 July 1848.

sarily be political, as blacks labored to make gains in education and employment. Douglass realized that politically directed abolitionism could accomplish that which moral suasion could not; it could procure universal emancipation and what Douglass termed "practical equality."

More than the natural equality of all humanity, a proposition that found expression in the philosophy of moral suasion, Douglass desired practical equality or equal attainment with whites. Moral suasion, without political agitation, was unable to accomplish equal attainment. Though Douglass did not despair of moral suasion as an effective principle, he certainly came to reject it as a primary means of attaining the overarching objectives of abolition and emancipation. Political activism seemed to promise a greater probability of satisfying his increasing stress on the need for tangible results.

THE *NORTH STAR* EDITORIALS

The *North Star* episode in Douglass's life generated his transition from moral suasion to political abolitionism, and that gave rise to the political emphasis in his moral thought, resulting in his concept of "particular responsibility." By claiming the particular responsibility to promote the elevation of blacks and not merely their emancipation, Douglass unavoidably surpassed the Garrisonian project. As editor of the *North Star*, he turned to the task of promoting black elevation and practical equality with whites.

Important indicators of the changes in Douglass's thought appeared in his editorials during of the 1850s. First, he attended more to political questions, and he linked political events of the day to national policies beyond slavery. Second, his interest in organized religion diminished and he distanced himself from the institutional church. His religious convictions remained strong as personal motivation, but their explicit role waned in his constructive thinking. Finally, he reacted energetically to several political setbacks in the 1850s, namely, the Fugitive Slave Act of 1850; the Kansas-Nebraska Act of 1854, and the Dred Scott

Decision of 1857.[6] These events, like the brutal floggings at the hands of Covey, inspired Douglass, provoked his anger, and strengthened his resolve.

Douglass devoted less attention to international affairs than to national ones among the political questions of the day. When he did refer to international events, it was usually to criticize the national government for its slaveholder's mentality in the treatment of other brown-skinned people. The most significant international event Douglass addressed between 1847 and 1851 was the war between the United States and Mexico. In an editorial from January 1848, Douglass identified the joint cause of the war with Mexico and slavery's war on blacks: "Mexico seems a doomed victim to Anglo-Saxon cupidity and love of dominion.... We have no preference for parties, regarding this slaveholding crusade."[7] In his assessment of the war as an act of American cupidity and dominion, and his denunciation of the conflict as an egregious act, Douglass combined value judgment with political assessment. The editorial treatment of the war was a harbinger of Douglass's political abolitionism.

On the national scene, Douglass revisited familiar topics, but his approach to them indicated the changes he had undergone. Take, for example, his understanding of the place of the US Constitution in the abolitionist struggle. In February 1849, Douglass created a great wave of interest as his readers detected that in one of his letters, reprinted as an editorial, he softened his strict Garrisonian position. In that letter, addressed to the political abolitionist C. H. Chase, Douglass distinguished between the letter of the document and the intentions of its framers:

> On a close examination of the Constitution, I am satisfied that if strictly "construed according to its reading," it is not a proslavery instrument... I now hold, as I have ever done, that the original intent and meaning

---

[6] The latter two events occurred after the *North Star* years. I include them here to present a more comprehensive account of the tumultuous 1850s.

[7] Frederick Douglass, "The War with Mexico," *North Star*, 21 January 1848

of the Constitution (the one given to it by the men who framed it, those who adopted, and the one given to it by the Supreme Court of the United States) makes it a proslavery instrument—such an one as I cannot bring myself to vote under, or swear to support.[8]

Chase was not alone in the belief that Douglass made a major concession to the political abolitionists. By separating the letter of the law from its spirit and original intent, Douglass indeed affirmed that the letter of the law was antislavery. But he maintained that the conceiving spirit and original intent of the Constitution made it a proslavery document in principle. His divergence from Garrison on this point is self-evident. Garrison made no such distinction between the letter of the law and its original intent.

If in his response Douglass distanced himself from Garrison, he also distanced himself from the political abolitionists. Although he conceded to the political abolitionists that the Constitution was antislavery in its wording, he held nonetheless that he could not support the document on moral grounds. It was a proslavery document in both its original intent and subsequent legal interpretation. Douglass believed that the Constitution endorsed both liberty and slavery, and that, according to God's will, "fidelity to the one is necessarily treachery to the other."[9] Political abolitionists such as Chase and Gerrit Smith cheered Douglass's rejection of Garrisonian superintendency. The Garrisonians were perplexed.

In the following month, Douglass distanced himself from the political abolitionists. On the issue of whether or not the Constitution ought to be abandoned, he reclaimed familiar territory. "We are not for mending old clothes with new clothes, or putting new wine into old bottles, but for starting afresh under a new and higher light than our piratical fathers saw, and form a Constitution

---

[8] Frederick Douglass, "Letter to C. H. Chase," *North Star*, 9 February 1849.

[9] Frederick Douglass, "Oath to Support the Constitution," *North Star*, 5 April 1850.

and government which shall be so clear and explicit that no doubt can be entertained as to its minutest purposes."[10]

For the next two years, Douglass straddled the ideological divide, siding with Gerrit Smith on the letter of the document and with Garrison on its interpretation. Though Smith's analysis weighed heavily, Garrison's absolutist ideals provided Douglass with a sturdy moral foundation. He struggled with his position for many years, a position that integrated the flexibility and effectiveness of political action with the rectitude and the zeal of Garrisonian moral suasion.

In a Garrisonian moment, Douglass explained to political abolitionists why he hesitated to abandon the earlier school of thought: "It is not enough that a man can demonstrate that his plan will abolish slavery to satisfy us that his plan is the right and best one to be adopted."[11] Moments like this one, however, became less frequent as he grew weary of conceding the Constitution to proslavery advocates. Specifically, Douglass resented that his position compelled him to argue, in accord with slaveholders, that the Fugitive Slave Act of 1850 was justified by a proslavery Constitution. A strict Garrisonian felt no anxiety about giving the Constitution to its rightful owners.[12] Douglass, on the other hand, showed an increasing unwillingness to jettison the political document.

The themes that I call *internal* are the most numerous and compelling of his editorials. They range from commentary on character and resistance, to racism, to colored schools and churches.[13] Insofar as the discussion of these internal themes were intended to create change in the black community from within, they addressed both a way of being (an ethic of character), and a

---

[10] Frederick Douglass, "Comments on Gerrit Smith's Address," *North Star*, 30 March 1849.

[11] Ibid.

[12] See chapter 3.

[13] The topics Douglass addressed portray his moral thought as it pertained to the emancipation and elevation of black people. Further, in analyzing these themes, we can perceive more readily how political considerations began to assume greater prominence in his moral thinking.

manner of doing (an ethic of action). Character and action, then, were the mainstay of Douglass's internal memoranda to the black community.

Douglass believed that character was one of two primary catalysts for equality, the second being noninterference from whites. Character generated equality by commanding the respect of one's oppressor and by increasing one's self-respect. Respect, in turn, cut against anti-black prejudice.

Douglass included industry, sobriety, honesty, and sound judgment among the other aspects of character.[14] These were universally compelling, "find them where you will, among black or white, [these] must be looked up to—can never be looked down upon."[15] Good character served as a leveling agent in society, producing mutual admiration among blacks and whites:

> Society, despite you and us, regulates itself; like water, it finds its level. In order, then, to blend into this element, our specific gravity should be equal. By this we mean to say, there are several qualifications entering into the combination of materials which compose society. These materials, from their nature, have an affinity for their like; hence, as attraction is mutual, materials of opposite qualities cannot adhere. Whatever qualifies and adorns society, must adorn and qualify us. We want education, trades, respectable employment, as merchants, farmers, and tradesmen in general. We can never rise to equality with the dominant class, while contented and satisfied with the situation of menials.[16]

In order to blend into white society, Douglass commended the imitation or adoption of character traits praised by those whites with whom blacks sought to integrate. This goal was not the imitation of whites as an end in itself, but to create a core of

---

[14] Frederick Douglass, "What Are the Colored People Doing for Themselves?"*North Star*, 14 July 1848.

[15] Ibid.

[16] Frederick Douglass, "Equality," *North Star*, 18 August 1848.

middle class blacks by adopting the values of middle class whites—values that were commendable on their own merit and not just for their utility. Without these values, Douglass feared that blacks would be stuck in menial positions and worse, that they would become contented to remain in menial positions. The key to the middle class, to Douglass's way of thinking, was as much in its values as in its vocations. Middle class whites would respond positively to the same values, the same character traits, reflected even in blacks. And once that occurred, vocational integration could proceed apace.

The upshot of Douglass's theory of character is the idea that given freedom, character trumps race as a condition for equality. An editorial dated 14 July 1848 gives credence to this interpretation. "With character," Douglass wrote, "we shall be powerful. Nothing can harm us long when we get character."[17] Character presented a variety of benefits to advancement: "In its presence, the sneers of a caricaturing press, the taunts of natural inferiority...are innoxious [sic], powerless, and unavailing. In answer to...the sneers of the multitude, there is nothing in the wide world half so effective as the presentation of a character precisely the opposite of all their representations."[18]

Though a necessary condition of elevation, character was not a sufficient condition. Blacks also had to become cognizant of the ways in which racism impeded their progress. More than merely its aggrandizing effect upon white people, racism induced despondency among black people. Hopelessness caused many blacks to acquiesce and to accept what they perceived as their lot in life. The greatest ally of character was self-consciousness. Douglass understood that raising the consciousness of blacks concerning white racism was an essential condition of elevation.

By educating blacks to what he called the "doctrine" of inferiority, Douglass believed that he fostered a heightened race-consciousness, which in turn enabled blacks to free themselves

---

[17] Frederick Douglass, "What Are the Colored People Doing for Themselves?" *North Star*, 14 July 1848.

[18] Ibid.

from the psychological effects of racism. Knowledge that the problem of race in America was not a black problem was the catalyst for blacks to cast off hopelessness. In an editorial on the doctrine of inferiority from September 1848, Douglass lamented the cost of imputed inferiority to black self-esteem:

> The doctrine perseveringly proclaimed in high places in church and state, that it is impossible for colored [people] to rise from ignorance and debasement, to intelligence and respectability in this country, has made a deep impression upon the public mind generally, and is not without its effect upon us. Under this gloomy doctrine, many of us have sunk under the pall of despondency, and are making no effort to relieve ourselves, and have no heart to assist others. It is from this despond that we would deliver you.[19]

Douglass hoped that blacks would throw off the psychological shackles resulting from slavery—shackles that bred defeatism and self-hatred—and resist their oppression in both attitude and action.

With middle-class values and heightened race-consciousness, Douglass argued that resistance was essential to elevation. He once remarked that it was better for black men to be beaten down by the police in defense of a fugitive slave than to relinquish the slave without resistance. The act of resistance affirmed the confluence of positive character traits and race-consciousness.

Middle-class values failed to promote elevation when undermined by self-loathing. If one believed herself best suited to menial work, then the presence of a virtuous character mandated only that she fulfill her role diligently and conscientiously. On the other hand, if blacks who resisted the doctrine of inferiority refused to develop those values and traits necessary for participation in an integrated middle-class society, then

---

[19] Frederick Douglass, "An Address to the Colored People of The United States," *North Star*, 22 September 1848.

progressive race-consciousness would also fail to achieve elevation. Successful elevation for blacks depended on a curious mix of assimilation and resistance; of integration and separation.

Some blacks, such as *North Star* co-editor Martin Delaney, proposed recolonization in Africa because they recognized that the doctrine of inferiority was a perpetual stumbling block to black elevation. Interestingly, Douglass opposed all calls for black recolonization, whether in Africa or in New Mexico.[20] Douglass understood that charting a geography of racial separation did not redress the racial divide between blacks and whites:

> This we take to be another cunning scheme of our oppressors. Once get the free colored man confined in any one territory or locality—let us once be separated from the white people of this country, and we shall become the mere game of American trappers and other adventurers, and there is no reason to believe our fate will be in any respect better than the noble Seminoles and other Indians who have perished by the perfidy and rapacity of the proud Anglo-Saxon race.... Nothing seems more evident to us, than that our destiny is sealed up with that of the white people of this country, and we believe that we must fall or flourish with them.[21]

Though Douglass admonished people of color to resist white racism, he did not sanction the separation of the races for fear that mere distance failed to end Anglo-Saxon domination. Douglass believed that the safest place for blacks was among whites.

Beyond this negative reason for integration, Douglass also embraced a deeper, positive rationale for integration. In noting the destiny of blacks was inextricably connected to that of whites, Douglass intimated that integration is a desirable course in its own right. He truly enjoyed his associations and friendships among

---

[20] Senator Hannegan of Indiana was one of the legislators who proposed the recolonization of blacks in New Mexico.

[21] Frederick Douglass, "A Few Words to Our Own People," *North Star*, 19 January 1849.

educated and cultured whites, and viewed interaction with whites on terms of equality as positive and conducive to elevation.

For these reasons, Douglass consistently opposed the establishment and perpetuation of black churches and schools. He believed that both were dangerous to the cause of black elevation insofar as they consolidated race-based separation.

As a realist, however, Douglass knew that blacks could not travel directly from the field to the middle-class, and so he proposed a black industrial college. His idea for an industrial college was not developed, but the idea itself revealed the balancing act that guided Douglass's strategy for elevation. Blacks needed a boost to enter the middle-class, and a race-based college could provide such assistance. For all its advantages, however, Douglass was still wary of race-based institutions, even those that helped blacks. He conceded that some were necessary, but he knew that integration was jeopardized if they became permanent.

The church serves as an example of his worst fears and Douglass had little positive to say about a race-based ecclesiology:

> We give it as our deliberate conviction that separate religious organizations, and "Negro pews" for the especial and exclusive use of colored persons, originated in most unholy and unnatural prejudices; that they are a mere counterpart of colonization, and that their existence is a serious injury to the best interests of the colored people, at variance with the glorious cause of liberty and human equality; and so far from being in accordance with the will or purposes of our Heavenly Father, they are diametrically opposed to the spirit and precepts of the gospel of Christ.[22]

Douglass wanted his readers to question the long term benefits and deficits of creating black institutions instead of fighting to integrate existing white institutions. He feared that permanent black institutions would ultimately fail to establish a

---

[22] Frederick Douglass, "Colored Churches," *North Star*, 25 February 1848.

black middle class that could integrate into the white middle class. Without integration, blacks would continue to be vulnerable to the economic and social effects of white racism. The benefits of black self-empowerment amounted to a Pyrrhic victory in the absence of a direct assault on institutionalized racism and racial prejudice.

Douglass's fears about the vulnerability of blacks were exacerbated by passage of the Fugitive Slave Act on 18 September 1850. The law requiring the return of fugitive slaves to their owners was a part of the Compromise of 1850. The Compromise consisted of five measures signed into law between 9–20 September of that year. The remaining four measures included the establishment of a territorial government in New Mexico, the admission of California as a free state, the organization of the Utah Territory, and the abolition of the slave trade in the District of Columbia.[23]

The Fugitive Slave Act took center stage for Douglass. It fell on the antislavery movement as the major challenge of the day and Douglass was disappointed in the movement as a whole for its lack of vigor in response to the bill. He complained that the antislavery movement was a "dry bones" movement lacking the spirit necessary to overturn the bill. In contrast to the uninspired response from the majority of the antislavery movement, Douglass was drawn to the vigorous opposition offered by the Liberty Party.

The Liberty Party was small and unpopular, but Douglass respected its eloquent and scholarly leader who was his friend and benefactor, Gerrit Smith. Beyond his attraction to the zeal of the party and his friendship with Smith, Douglass found the Liberty Party attractive for several other reasons. Of the various antislavery organizations that were active at the time, the Liberty Party came closest to the kind of balance between political action and moral suasion that Douglass sought to create. The Liberty Party also showed an interest in collaborating with Douglass rather than merely absorbing him into their ranks. The other organizations in the movement made no partnership offers that

---

[23] *The Frederick Douglass Papers*, ed. John W. Blassingame. 5 vols. (New York: Yale University Press, 1979) 2:259.

would have allowed Douglass to maintain his journalistic autonomy.

Though Douglass was leaning toward the Liberty Party for its principles, it took an offer of financial assistance from Gerrit Smith in 1851 to bring Douglass completely into the organization's camp. In June 1851 the *North Star* merged with the *Liberty Party Paper* to become *Frederick Douglass' Paper*.

The *North Star* years depict Douglass as a man in transition. I understand those years as transformative ones in that they found him torn between Garrison and the Liberty Party, evaluating alternate abolitionist approaches and discerning what it meant to be a black abolitionist. Douglass launched his editorial enterprise by accepting the responsibility of advocacy for the black community and he struggled to make good on that responsibility. Within four years, he endorsed those beliefs and principles that disclosed his mature thought.

FREDERICK DOUGLASS' PAPER

Douglass found his stride in the columns of his new paper. At the beginning of his career in public speaking, he had adopted the Garrisonian belief system, albeit with some reservations. Later, he chose the Liberty Party because its strategy compared favorably to the other antislavery organizations. In 1841, the American Anti-Slavery Society informed his beliefs about effecting emancipation. In 1851, it was his beliefs about effecting emancipation that led him to the Liberty Party.

The influence of both Garrison and Smith was evident in the first edition of Douglass's new paper: "In respect to the church and the government, we especially wish to make ourselves fully and clearly understood. With the religion of one and the politics of the other, our soul shall have no communion. These we regard as central pillars in the horrid temple of slavery."[24] By disavowing the corruption of both church and government, Douglass faced the

---

[24] Editorial, Frederick Douglass, *Frederick Douglass' Paper*, 26 June 1851.

immediate problem of establishing himself as a credible voice within the existing American religious and political realms.

During the first few months of the new paper's publication, Douglass defended his conversion to the Liberty Party and spelled out in detail his view on the Constitution, the Fugitive Slave Act, and a host of other familiar issues. His critics, however, were not satisfied. They assailed his latest journalistic effort as little more than an organ of the Liberty Party and questioned his integrity. For his part, Douglass met the criticisms with lucid and cogent arguments in support of his new positions.

In defense of his conversion to the Liberty Party, Douglass showed that he was more of an eclectic theorist than his Garrisonian peers. In contrast to Garrison's absolutist approach to emancipation, Douglass argued the efficacy of a consequentialist approach to emancipation, and beyond emancipation, to practical equality. Take the matter of the US Constitution, for example. Both Douglass and Garrison understood the document to protect slaveholding interests, and both men were opposed to that protection. They differed about how best to act on their opposition. Garrison took an absolutist position. By that I mean to say, he argued that the Constitution should be nullified, regardless of the consequences resulting from nullification. Douglass believed that nullification was bad policy because the consequences from such a measure would compromise the goal of emancipation. Douglass's opinion of how best to act in opposition to the Constitution was determined by the value of the consequences of such action. Garnering propositions from several editorials written in July 1851, I will reconstruct the basic argument that most closely approximates Douglass's defense of emancipation. Douglass interweaved deontological and consequentialist claims, as well as Christian religious and secular claims, to make what seemed to him the most compelling argument.

The simplest argument from Douglass's numerous writings on emancipation is rooted in claims of human freedom. Douglass asserted that the claims of human freedom were "imperative, immediate, and incapable of postponement."[25] Freedom was an urgent need, because corporate wrongdoing and the suffering that it produced were so entrenched. More than merely a need, however, freedom was also an obligation. The moral agent had a duty to carry the principle of human freedom "into all the relations of life, at home or abroad, in the church, or in the street everywhere."[26] Douglass argued that the moral agent had a duty to fight for freedom wherever oppression existed.

Though he did not author the edict, "by any means necessary," Douglass believed that any and all reasonable strategies for freedom were authorized by their end. He wrote, "Everything in morals, religion and politics, which can reasonably be made available to the grand consummation ought to be seized upon without hesitation."[27] Barring erratic and arbitrary acts of retaliatory violence, Douglass defended a comprehensive and multivalent strategy for accomplishing emancipation. Sympathizers of the movement to emancipate slaves need not share particular ideological or religious stances. They were not limited to protesting the condition of blacks in narrowly prescribed idioms, or required to endorse the same methods for correcting the blight of slavery. What they needed was commitment, a strategy, and a willingness to coalesce with other sympathizers into a united front against slavery. Douglass took on the Garrisonians, for example, for failing to use political agitation and other viable weapons in the war against slavery.

Douglass's polemic against the sufficiency of moral suasion as an effective avenue to achieve emancipation was based on a principle of action that he derived from scripture. Douglass argued that the Old Testament endorsed political action. He favored the biblical idea of the day when every one "sits under his own vine

---

[25] Frederick Douglass, "The Liberty Party Call," *Frederick Douglass' Papers*, 31 July 1851.

[26] Ibid.

[27] Frederick Douglass, "Is the US Constitution For or Against Slavery?," *Frederick Douglass' Paper*, 24 July 1851.

and fig tree, and eats the fruits of his own labor."[28] Douglass grounded his justification of political action in this verse on the principle that "the highest civil, is [also] the highest religious condition."[29]

This principle became the basis of Douglass's ethic of action. He claimed that political action was a necessary condition of emancipation on religious grounds. Accept for the moment that there is indeed proportionality between the religious and political realms. The concept in question, then, contained a political corollary, namely, an affirmation of "the common rights of all [people] not to liberty only," but to enjoy the fruits of their own labor.[30] Since common rights fell under the protection of civil government, it was incumbent on moral agents to ensure that civil government acted to protect the common rights of all persons. This duty, buttressed by religious argument, justified the agent in her use of political action because it was the means best suited to civil reform.

Douglass challenged those insisting on the sole use of moral suasion to counter slavery and the emerging racism of the day with a religious justification (a moral equivalent) for political action. In an editorial dated 23 March 1855, he criticized the Garrisonian battle cry, "no union with slaveholders." He wrote, "As a mere expression of abhorrence of slavery, the sentiment is a good one; but it expresses no intelligible principle of action, and throws no new light on the pathway of duty."[31] He chided the Garrisonians for a failure of moral duty, owing to the lack of an intelligible ethic of action:

----

[28] Frederick Douglass, "The Liberty Party Platform," Frederick Douglass's Paper, 31 July 1851. Douglass writes: "The highest civil, is the highest religious condition. The Bible means it, when every man 'sits under his own vine and fig tree, and eats the fruits of his own labor.' It is not only a religious, but a political condition also.

[29] Frederick Douglass, "The Liberty Party Platform," Frederick Douglass' Paper, 31 July 1851..

[30] Ibid.

[31] Frederick Douglass, "The Anti-Slavery Movement: A Lecture by Frederick Douglass before the Rochester Ladies' Anti-Slavery Society," Frederick Douglass' Paper, 23 March 1855.

> But again; no union with slaveholders. I dislike the morality of this sentiment... For instance: A. unites with B. in stealing my property, and carrying it away to California or to Australia, and while there, Mr. A. becomes convinced that he did wrong in stealing my property, and says to Mr. B. "no union with property stealers," and abandons him, leaving the property in his hands. Now, I put it to this audience, has Mr. A. in this transaction, met the requirements of stringent morality? He, certainly, has not. It is not only his duty to separate from the thief but to restore the stolen property to its rightful owner. And I hold that in the Union, this very thing of restoring to the slave his long lost rights can better be accomplished, than it can possibly be accomplished outside of the Union.[32]

Emancipation alone was not enough. Restoration of the common rights that civil government denied to blacks was necessary to liberty and exceeded the call for mere emancipation.

Douglass was not deaf to the argument that the Garrisonian method was more effective in converting people to antislavery righteousness, nor to the argument that political action only encouraged people to participate in an intrinsically evil system. Douglass responded that the arguments were true if, and only if, the Garrisonians showed "that refusing to vote does something to increase their moral power."[33] On the contrary, Douglass maintained that the efficacy of antislavery preaching by a nonvoter over against that of a voter was not self-evident. The politically active antislavery agent need not concede ground to the nonvoting moralist on the basis of transforming souls. Douglass asserted that the proof of ideological "superiority" rested in empirical evidence and not in an *a priori* judgment based upon doctrinal preference.

---

[32] Ibid.

[33] Frederick Douglass, "The Superiority of Moral over Political Action," *Frederick Douglass' Paper*, 3 December 1852.

If civil and religious law mandated political action in the defense of common rights, then the US Constitution, as the embodiment of national law, was an essential document for abolitionists to take as their own. The Constitution, by definition, did not abrogate that which it was ordained to establish, namely, liberty, justice and the general good. These ends involved the protection of the common rights of all citizens, rights that Douglass identified as the God-given, common rights of all humanity. Therefore, the Constitution could not authorize slavery even if the framers intended it to do so. He wrote: "It is a fundamental truth that every man is the rightful owner of his own body. If you have no right to the possession of another man's body your fathers had no such right. But suppose that they have written in a constitution that they have a right, you and I have no right to conform to it."[34]

Douglass argued extensively from his first great principle, that the highest civil is [also] the highest religious condition. He concluded from its application that civil government was legitimate to the extent that it protected the common rights granted humanity by God in nature; that the protection of those rights warranted the use of political action; and finally, that the principle of action conformed to moral duty, or what Douglass termed the requirements of stringent morality.[35]

This grand, religio-political principle influenced Douglass's political views even as it influenced his epistemology. In an era of sweeping reform, Douglass understood political reform as corollary to the religious virtue of righteousness. In a speech delivered at a Democratic convention in Ithaca, New York, also printed as an editorial in his paper, Douglass voiced his guiding political principle: "I have one great political idea... That idea is an old idea. It is widely and generally assented to; nevertheless, it is very generally trampled upon and disregarded. The best

---

[34] Frederick Douglass, "National Free Soil Convention," reprinted from the *New York Tribune* in *Frederick Douglass' Paper*, 20 August 1852.

[35] Frederick Douglass, "The Anti-Slavery Movement: A Lecture by Frederick Douglass before the Rochester Ladies' Anti-Slavery Society," *Frederick Douglass's Paper*, 23 March 1855.

expression of it I have found in the Bible. It is in substance, 'righteousness exalteth a nation—sin is a reproach to any people.' This constitutes my politics, the negative and positive of my politics, and the whole of my politics."[36] Douglass conferred normative value to the principle in holding that "whatever rights or privileges may be enjoyed innocently by white [people], may as innocently be enjoyed by [people] of color."[37] Race simply was not a relevant criterion in the establishment and distribution of societal benefits and burdens.

Douglass believed that the moral agent was obligated to resist oppression in defense of the natural and inalienable common rights of humanity. Not only an index of character, resistance also bore political meaning and significance. The right of resistance[38] followed from his principle of action, as well as from his account of character. Douglass considered resistance a valuable character trait and also a viable form of political action. Whenever the subject of the Fugitive Slave Law was raised, Douglass asserted the slave's right of resistance. On one such occasion, during a speech at Pittsburgh, Douglass explained how the right of resistance should be utilized in opposition to the recapturing of fugitive slaves:

> The only way to make the Fugitive Slave Law a dead letter is to make half a dozen or more dead kidnappers. A half dozen more dead kidnappers carried down south would cool the ardor of Southern gentlemen, and keep their rapacity in check. That is perfectly right as long as the colored man has no protection.... I believe that the lines of eternal justice are sometimes so obliterated by a course of long continued oppression that it is necessary to

---

[36] Frederick Douglass, "Speech of Frederick Douglass, Delivered at the Mass Free Democratic Convention at Ithaca on Thursday, October 14th," *Frederick Douglass' Paper*, 22 October 1852.

[37] Frederick Douglass, "Jaunt to Cincinnati," *Frederick Douglass' Paper*, 13 May 1852.

[38] Frederick Douglass, "Spirit of Cincinnati Press in Regards to the Anti-Slavery Convention," *Frederick Douglass' Paper*, 6 May 1852.

revive them by deepening their traces with the blood of a tyrant.[39]

Though severe, the call to physical resistance was consistent with Douglass's understanding of moral duty. His logic is clear. If defense of the common rights of humanity was a moral duty, if political action was a requirement of moral duty, and if physical resistance was a reasonable method of political action, then physical resistance was a morally permissible method of political action so long as it is undertaken in defense of the common rights of humanity.

Douglass's logic on resistance is expressed most clearly in an editorial dated 2 June 1854 titled, "Is it Right and Wise to Kill a Kidnapper?" He wrote the editorial five months after the introduction of the Nebraska Bill into the Senate by Stephen A. Douglas, and approximately three days after its passage. The Kansas-Nebraska Act nullified the regulations of the Missouri Compromise that restricted the extension of slavery into the old Louisiana Purchase. It also reinforced the principle of congressional nonintervention with slavery already practiced in the territory.[40] Responding to this political setback, Douglass outlined what he believed to be an original approach to the problems caused by the Fugitive Slave Act and the Kansas-Nebraska Act. "Our moral philosophy on this point is our own—never having read what others may have said in favor of the views which we entertain...."[41] The structure of his argument confirms the disclaimer. Yet, Douglass did have something worthwhile to say about the justifiability of violence when engaged in self-defense.

At face value it would seem that killing one engaged in enforcing the Fugitive Slave Law constitutes murder. Douglass, however, argued in four propositions that such an act amounted to

---

[39] Frederick Douglass, "National Free Soil Convention," *Frederick Douglass' Paper*, 20 August 1852.

[40] *The Frederick Douglass Papers*, ed. John W. Blassingame et al. 5 vols. (New York: Yale University Press, 1979) 2:464.

[41] Frederick Douglass, "Is it Right and Wise to Kill a Kidnapper?," *Frederick Douglass' Paper*, 2 June 1854.

a justified killing. First, he denied an absolute right to life. There are conditions under which one can be justifiably deprived of one's right to life. Second, these conditions are derived from nature. As one can be justly deprived of one's right to liberty in accord with the laws of nature, so one can also be justly deprived of one's right to life. Third, society has the right to preserve itself even at the expense of the life of an aggressor. Finally, the individual has a right of self-defense even at the expense of the life of an aggressor.

Douglass derived the first proposition from reflections on the purpose of life. He theorized that life's end is one's "own good" and the honor of God.[42] The purpose of life was to fulfill that end. Life, therefore, was ordered to a higher end. No right can be claimed that in any way mitigates the end for which life was designed.[43] The moral agent can claim a right to life, but that right remained ancillary to the unique veneration the moral agent owes God. Should the right to life ever conflict with the purpose of life, then the moral agent was obligated to relinquish claims to the former in order to satisfy the demands of the latter. For that reason, the right to life was not an absolute right. It was always conditional, always dependent on that which one owed to God.

The second proposition derived from premises that followed from the first. Given that there was no absolute right to life, then life, like all other human rights, could be forfeited in certain circumstances and justly taken away. Douglass theorized that the right to life "stands on the same ground as the right to liberty," and is subject to "all the exceptions that apply to the right of liberty."[44] If one accepted the comparison, then it followed that society could regulate life even as it regulates liberty. One's liberty can be abrogated if one denied another's liberty. So too with life, Douglass argued.

Douglass's transition to the third proposition, clear in and of itself, is a bit tricky. Douglass inferred from the second propo-

---

[42] Ibid.
[43] Ibid.
[44] Ibid.

sition that the authority to take a life rests with society, which has the right of self-preservation. He stated that without a right to take life, "a single individual would have it in his power to destroy the peace and the happiness of ten thousand otherwise right-minded people."[45] Society, therefore, responded against perpetrators with capital punishment when life was taken unjustly. Capital punishment might also be used when absolutely necessary to maintain the peace essential to society's self-preservation.

Making the transition a bit confusing, Douglass grounded the societal right to take life in the law of justice that is deduced from nature. The law of justice can be thought of as the guiding principle of the moral realm. It operated much like the laws of physics. When a person committed suicide, for example, she forfeited her right to life according to the laws of the physical world. Similarly, when a person committed homicide, she forfeited her right to life according to the laws of the moral and social world that issued the law of justice.

By deftly extending the definition of homicide—the killing of one person by another—to include slavery, Douglass argued that those who "take pleasure in enslaving, imbruting, and murdering their fellow men," were subject to the laws of the moral world in the same way that those who committed suicide were subject to the laws of the physical world.[46] They have, by their activity, forfeited the right to life and deserve to die according to the laws of nature.

In the fourth proposition, Douglass extended to individuals the right to take life. When civil government failed to protect the life of an individual from an aggressor, then the individual could claim the same right as society, the right of self-preservation. In the individual, this right is called the right of self-defense. It entitled the individual to do in her own defense that which society rightly did in its defense. The upshot is that fugitive slaves had a right to kill those who tried to return them to slavery. Slave catchers, by the very nature of their occupation, forfeited their

---

[45] Ibid.
[46] Ibid.

right to life. So long as they acted in self-defense, fugitive slaves were justified by the laws of the moral and social world in taking the lives of slave catchers. By their oppressive actions against fellow human beings, slave catchers forfeited the right to life.

Physical resistance against slavery was also attractive to Douglass for other reasons. Though he clearly accepted a political defense of physical resistance, Douglass saw resistance as a leading indicator of character, of what he deemed "manliness." Blacks needed to resist slavery because it was good for the soul. Resistance to slavery, to the Fugitive Slave Law, to re-colonization, and to all other indices of white racism developed "manliness," or perhaps stated differently, confident self-reliance in blacks. In a rhetorical question raised in an editorial on African re-colonization, Douglass wondered how long blacks would acquiesce to white domination: "When will our people learn that they have the power to crush this viper which is stinging our very life away? And still more, when will they have the energy, the nerve and manliness to use it?"[47]

The interplay between character and action sowed the seeds of Douglass's understanding of self-help. Self-help was not only an admirable value, but also constituted an act of resistance. It held both moral and political significance for Douglass. Self-help commanded some of his most vehement language. In fact, Douglass grew more vehement in his message of black self-help while the editor of *Frederick Douglass' Paper* than as editor of the *North Star*. Beyond the forceful insistence of the message, Douglass also proposed a viable method of self-help in the creation of an industrial college for blacks. The boldness of the message and the introduction of a specific proposal to address the dire need distinguished Douglass's treatment of the theme from that of the earlier *North Star* years.

An editorial from March 1853 titled "Learn Trades or Starve!" illuminates not only the tone of Douglass's appeal to

---

[47] Frederick Douglass, "African Colonization," *Frederick Douglass' Paper*, 31 July 1851.

blacks, but also his assessment of how character informed action. The following excerpt serves to illustrate:

> As a black man, we say if we cannot stand up, let us fall down. We desire to be a man among men while we do live; and when we cannot, we wish to die. It is evident, painfully evident to every reflecting mind, that the means of living, for colored men, are becoming more and more precarious and limited. Employments and callings, formerly monopolized by us, are so no longer.... Without the means of living, life is a curse, and leaves us at the mercy of the oppressor to become his debased slaves.[48]

Douglass aptly put his finger on an exigent problem facing free blacks. Freedom without the means of survival, without meaningful employment, was a revolving door to powerlessness. If powerlessness was the problem, then action was the solution:

> Now, colored men, what do you mean to do, for you must do something? The American Colonization Society tells you to go to Liberia. Mr. Bibb tells you to go to Canada. Others tell you to go to school. We tell you to go to work; and to work you must go or DIE. Men are not valued in this country, or in any country, for what they are; they are valued for what they can do.... We must show that we can do as well as be; and to this end we must learn trades.[49]

As a consequence of his work ethic, Douglass favored vocation over education as the starting point for black elevation. In a March 1853 editorial he held that "the means of living must precede education."[50] Douglass reasoned that education was ancillary

---

[48] Frederick Douglass, "Learn Trades Or Starve!," *Frederick Douglass' Paper*, 4 March 1853.

[49] Ibid.

[50] Frederick Douglass, "A Few More Words about Learning Trades," *Frederick Douglass' Paper*, 11 March 1853.

to vocation for two main reasons. First and foremost, education alone was incapable of surmounting the barriers of racial discrimination. Free black parents who struggled to provide their children with higher education often saw those children return home unable to find work in skilled positions. Douglass asked, "Can the daughters find schools to teach? Or the sons find books to keep? Do abolitionists give them employment in their stores or counting-houses?"[51] Better to train black children, Douglass thought, to become skilled artisans or farmers.

Second, educated blacks met with barriers among their own people. As Douglass put it, "[she] is equally cast out by the ignorance of the blacks."[52] Educated blacks were often shunned in their communities as traitors to the cause of racial uplift, and for associating with whites. Though formal education remained secondary to vocation for Douglass, he did not despair of the day when education would become equally important. He believed that, in time, a working class would generate an educated class among blacks. Actually, Douglass made the stronger claim that blacks would never have an educated class until and unless they had "more [people] of means" among them.[53]

Finally, the excerpt from "Learn Trades or Starve!" indicates Douglass's recognition that free black people in America needed an industrial college. His call for a black industrial college did not imply that he changed his mind regarding single race institutions. Douglass remained a committed integrationist but recognized that the sons and daughters of slaves needed a boost if they were to integrate with middle-class whites. His call for an industrial college should be understood as a means of facilitating elevation, integration, and practical equality with whites.

In a letter to Harriet Beecher Stowe, Douglass laid out the reasons for and benefits to be derived from the creation of such an institution. Citing poverty, ignorance, and degradation as the

---

[51] Ibid.

[52] Frederick Douglass, "Learn Trades or Starve," *Frederick Douglass' Paper*, 4 March 1853.

[53] Frederick Douglass, "A Few More Words about Learning Trades," *Frederick Douglass' Paper*, 11 March 1853.

combined ills of the "social disease" afflicting the free black community, Douglass reasoned that any effective cure had to address each of the three ailments. He rejected higher education and farming as viable options. The problem with higher education was its lack of acceptance in both black and white communities. Farming was unlikely because, as Douglass put it, "it is almost impossible to get colored men to go on the land."[54] The recognition that blacks migrated in large numbers to towns and cities led Douglass to conclude that the solution must have its basis in an urban environment.

Further, the solution had to increase self-reliance. More than any other consequence of the slave system, Douglass viewed the lack of self-reliance among blacks as the greatest loss suffered. Forced dependency on whites destroyed black initiative, which in turn destroyed the desire to succeed.

Douglass therefore proposed an industrial college in which training in the "mechanic arts" was combined with a "mental education."[55] He favored this type of institution for several reasons. First, it created the means for blacks to earn an honest living. Second, it provided practical knowledge. Third, it enabled blacks to develop and to demonstrate self-reliance. For these reasons, Douglass considered an industrial college dedicated to training blacks indispensable to the cause of that community's elevation into a society dominated by whites.

European immigration also contributed to the need for an industrial college for American blacks. Increasingly, poor Europeans replaced slaves and free blacks in such traditionally black jobs as coachman, waiter, barber, whitewasher, boot-blacker, steward, stevedore, and wood-sawyer.[56] Douglass hoped that an industrial college would open new sources of self-support for blacks and forge new channels of industry, alleviating the growing competition with Europeans as unskilled laborers.

---

[54] Frederick Douglass, "Letter to Mrs. Stowe," *Frederick Douglass' Paper*, 2 December 1853.

[55] Ibid.

[56] Frederick Douglass, "The Industrial College," *Frederick Douglass' Paper*, 20 January 1854.

Beyond appraisals of character and action, Douglass also enlisted anthropological reflection in his efforts against slavery. In July 1854 he delivered the commencement address at Western Reserve College on the topic of "The Claims of the Negro Race, Viewed in a Psychological and Physiological Light." The lecture, reprinted in his editorial columns, began as a response to an article published in the *Richmond Enquirer*. The issue at hand was the debased humanity of slaves. On one side of the issue, theorists like Samuel George Morton, 1799–1851, argued that Africans had smaller brains than Europeans. The argument was used to justify the claim that genetics and not slavery was finally responsible for the moral and social status of slaves. Based on his investigation of skulls in the 1830s and 1840s, Morton adopted the theory of a diverse origin of the human race. On the other side of the issue, Douglass argued that slaves were degraded by slavery. He refuted Morton's work in comparative craniology because it legitimated racist claims that blacks were not fully human.

For his part, Douglass argued contra Morton that the human race was born in Africa.[57] He asserted the unity of all Africans on the basis of philological investigations. He dispelled claims that civilization was born north of the Sahara among a people who were not black: "I affirm that one of the most direct and conclusive proofs of the general affinity of northern African nations, with those of West, East and South Africa, is found in the general similarity of their language. The philologist easily discovers, and is able to point out something like the original source of the multiplied tongues now in use in that yet mysterious quarter of the globe."[58] Douglass believed that Africans were originally one people who migrated to various parts of the continent. He also believed that they were not originally white people because not even the Egyptians, the custodians of ancient

---

[57] Frederick Douglass, "Something New," reprinted from the *Richmond Inquirer* in *Frederick Douglass's Paper*, 25 August 1854.

[58] Editorial, "The Claims of the Negro Race, Viewed in a Psychological and Physiological Light,", *Frederick Douglass' Paper*, 21 July 1854. This editorial was first presented as an address at Western Reserve College, 12 July 1854.

civilization, were white. According to Morton, Egyptians possessed brown complexions, rounded and wide nostrils, thick lips, and black and curly hair.[59] "A man in our day" with such features, Douglass added sarcastically, "would have no difficulty in getting himself recognized as a negro." If civilization was born of black parents, then how could respected journals like the *Richmond Enquirer* deny that blacks were fully human? This address by Douglass enjoyed increasing popularity.

THE *DOUGLASS MONTHLY* (1858–1863)

For all of his effort as an editor and orator, by the late 1850s abolitionism had proved a disappointment to Douglass. Contrary to his own higher expectations, the great political debate on slavery was little more than a genteel conversation on how far the "peculiar institution" would be allowed to extend. Abolitionists all but abandoned the fiery exhortations and persuasive pleas that had earlier defined the movement. By 1859 his discontent with the political debates found voice in his monthly:

> Abolitionism has become so attenuated, by the mixture of "non-extension" that there is but little of strength remaining. We do believe most sincerely that before there shall be much hope for the slave, the abolitionists must return to the old method of preaching. The slave and the slave's wrongs must be brought vividly before the people, and the deep wickedness of slaveholding must be pressed upon the heart and conscience.[60]

These Garrisonian sentiments returned to Douglass's writing with increasing frequency. He maintained that political abolitionism needed a good stiff dose of Garrisonian moral suasion to

---

[59] Ibid.
[60] Frederick Douglass, "The Signs of the Times," *Douglass' Monthly*, February, 1859, 21.

get it back up to speed. But on the eve of war between the American South and North, his call for a return to the old ways, for a united front against slavery, fell on deaf ears.

Though unheeded in his day, Douglass's call remains important, if for a reason different than that which he considered critical. The call sheds light on the shift that occurred in his fundamental approach to abolition. At one time a committed Garrisonian, and later a committed advocate of Gerrit Smith's political abolitionism, Douglass never fully abandoned either approach to emancipation. As tempting as it is to describe Douglass as a political abolitionist with strong Garrisonian leanings, that description is not entirely accurate. Moral suasion was more for Douglass than merely a tactic that could advance the cause of political abolition. It remained a principle as important as the principle of political action. Douglass believed that the wickedness of slavery had to be pressed upon the "heart and conscience" of the people because such knowledge was of salvific import; it could redeem hard hearts and calcified consciences in a way that politics could not duplicate. This is a Garrisonian argument if ever there was one.

Douglass never fully resolved the tension between the two approaches. He argued at times that the hearts and consciences of whites had to be troubled if emancipation was to become a reality, while maintaining at other times that "a good revolver, a steady hand, and a determination" to kill or to be killed in defense of freedom was the "true remedy" for slavery.[61] The tension is evident in his social ethics. Douglass endorsed both physical resistance and integration. He doubted that whites would advance the cause of justice without continued agitation from blacks, yet he believed nonetheless that blacks should accept the assistance of white sympathizers.

Apart from the topic of abolition reform, Douglass's moral themes remained constant with the earlier period. Universal suffrage, women's rights, self-help, education, and opposition to

---

[61] Frederick Douglass, "The True Remedy for the Fugitive Slave Bill," *Frederick Douglass' Paper*, 9 June 1854.

racism continued in his later columns. Douglass's editorials during this period demonstrated a certainty that surpassed mere conviction, as if he believed his insights were self-evident. Further, he wrote with a simplicity that revealed a high level of comfort and confidence in his grasp of the message, and in his role as a messenger.

Taking race relations as an example, Douglass went beyond condemnation of racism. He explained the hatred of blacks that undergirded racism: "We may be too sensitive, but it does seem to us that there is much of negro hatred to be abolished, even among those who call themselves antislavery men and women. Somehow the thought and feeling has obtained among them, that the negro does not suffer by being trodden upon, as does his proud white brother."[62]

His sensitivity to the dynamics of race relations in America also enabled him to perceive the grand deception that separated Southern white non-slaveholders and black slaves, both of whom had a common interest in the extirpation of slavery. He said of the non-slaveholding white South:

> They are depressed, oppressed, robbed, despised, neglected, and stripped of all social and political power...By the cunning of the slaveholders, the "poor white trash" (as the nonslaveholders are called,) are made to believe that the abolition of slavery would be to place the white laborer on a level with the negro. They will yet learn that such abolition would place the white laborer upon an equal footing with the slaveholder...[63]

Douglass's prognosis proved incorrect. Abolition did not create the conditions he expected, yet his diagnosis of the problem remains fascinating. By citing hatred of the negro, powerlessness, and class-based economic exploitation as indices of racism,

---

[62] Frederick Douglass, "The Signs of the Times," *Douglass' Monthly*, February, 1859, 21.

[63] Frederick Douglass, "The Impending Crisis of the South," *Douglass' Monthly*, February, 1859, 22.

Douglass strengthened his earlier position. His willingness to synthesize elements from various theories, and to extract from them those ideas that made a deep im-pression whether or not they could be readily integrated into his own, indicates an intellectual curiosity and ingenuity that continue to distinguish Douglass from among his con-temporaries.

On the issues of universal suffrage and equal school rights, for example, Douglass profited from noting a connection between the two. In opposition to many of his colleagues who argued that the battle for universal suffrage must precede the fight for school integration, Douglass argued that equal school rights, once ob-tained, created the conditions for universal suffrage. His rationale was based on the conviction that equality was "the best means to abolish caste."[64] If they procured the practical equality of school children, abolitionists could then gain equal suffrage with little effort. "If we obtain equal school rights," he argued, "the boon will be so radical that equal suffrage will follow as a matter of course."[65]

Douglass contended further that the battle for equal school rights was an easier fight than was that for universal suffrage. The battle for equal school rights issued from justice in taxation. Blacks paid taxes as did whites and therefore owned "an equal share in the school fund." Yet, blacks found that they were usually "debarred from equal school privileges."[66] The tax issue was central to the school rights debate.

Douglass became increasingly aware of the obstacles that had to be overcome if the reforms that he sought were to be realized. He had keen insight into the scope of the problems facing America. "It is easy," he wrote, "to discern the signs of the times,

---

[64] Frederick Douglass, "Equal Suffrage or Equal School Rights," *Douglass' Monthly*, March, 1859, 37.

[65] Ibid.

[66] Frederick Douglass, "The Suffrage and Education Questions," *Douglass' Monthly*, March, 1859, 33.

but to change them requires more than human power."[67] Douglass's characteristic optimism began to wane.

Taken as a whole, the signs of the era immediately preceding the war between the states were so grim that Douglass feared only God could bring about transformation. Douglass perceived the hand of God in the advent of war. What were the signs that evoked ever more melancholy in Douglass? Slavery and its concomitant racism composed one sign. The corruption of the church—both Northern and Southern—and the defilement of God's Word was another. Economic exploitation and gender discrimination comprised other signs of systemic injustice. The growing lack of comity between North and South, and continuing disingenuousess on the part of America's political parties were yet other signs of the era. So, too, was the needless violence that pervaded daily life.

Considered collectively, the signs disclose salient features of the American character in that period. Douglass thought that the rapid growth of the nation wreaked havoc on the national character, resulting in a fundamental disregard for life. In a column on American civilization, he speculated on the cultural effects of rapid growth.

This peculiarly American carelessness in the protection of life appears still more strikingly in the almost undisturbed freedom allowed to rowdyism. In fact, rowdyism is itself a plant of genuine American growth; for however wild, coarse and rude the mob may be in other countries, they do stand in fear of the law.... Part of this defect may be properly ascribed to the astonishing rapidity of its growth. Everywhere else, civilization was the result of an internal process, slow in its progress, taking deep root, modifying, shaping and governing life in all its ramifications. Here it comes like a whirlwind, sweeping over the land unequally....[68]

[67] Frederick Douglass, "The Signs of the Times," *Douglass' Monthly*, February, 1859, 21.

[68] Frederick Douglass, "American Civilization," *Douglass' Monthly*, October, 1859, 150.

This defect in the American character, a fundamental lack of concern for life, caused in part by rapid growth and rampant expansion, was evident not only in acts of mob violence but also in the workings of national government. Douglass cited the Fugitive Slave Act, the Kansas-Nebraska Act, and the Supreme Court rulings in the Dred Scott as examples of the peculiar American breed of rowdyism that did not yield to law, but sanctioned and interpreted law.

Douglass identified slavery as the truest and most critical test of the American character:

> Slavery is the great test question of our age and nation. It, above all others, enables us to draw the line between the precious and the vile, whether in individuals, creeds, sects, or parties. It marks, with the distinctiveness of summer-lightening upon a black cloud, the point dividing common honesty from knavery, benevolence from selfishness, magnanimity from meanness, elevation from baseness, moral courage from cowardice, sincere devotion from half-hearted and hypocritical pretension, "pure religion and undefiled," from a corrupt, putrid and dead religion, having no beneficent relation to the "age and body of the times" in which it exists.[69]

While his willingness to "separate the wheat from the chaff" was not new in 1859, his language revealed a change in perspective. Douglass had reached a new point in his development.

The Douglass of the early 1860s expressed the angst and dolefulness characteristic of military leaders who sustain heavy losses against a revitalized enemy. In a telling editorial written in August 1860, "The Prospect in the Future," Douglass ended one chapter in his life and began another. It deserves a quote of length:

---

[69] Frederick Douglass, "The True Test," *Douglass' Monthly*, July, 1859, 98.

The future of the antislavery cause is shrouded in doubt and gloom. The labors of a quarter of a century, instead of culminating in success, seem to have reached a point of weary hopelessness, so far as radical abolitionists are concerned. The great work of enlightening the people as to the wicked enormities of slavery, is well nigh accomplished, but the practical results of this work have disappointed our hopes. The grim and bloody tragedies of outrage and cruelty are rehearsed day by day to the ears of the people, but they look on as coolly indifferent as spectators in a theatre.... They assent to all the horrid truths which reveal the inhuman secrets of the gloomy prison house, but are not moved to action. They command the iron-linked logic, and soul-born eloquence of abolitionists, but never practice the principles laid bare by the one, or act upon the emotions called up by the other.... You cannot relate a new fact, or frame an un-familiar argument on this subject. Reason and morality have emptied their casket of richest jewels into the lap of this cause, in vain. Religion has exhausted her volleyed thunder of denunciation upon the head of this gigantic crime, but it stands unmoved and defiant.... Our courage, our love of liberty, our statesmanship, our literature, our ethics, and our religion, are all most intensely and wickedly selfish.[70]

The American character proved itself to be inordinately self-centered and self-justifying. The overarching moral case against slavery was ultimately impotent to weaken the selfishness that impeded the moral agents' receptivity.

Though Douglass continued to publish into the war, his writings no longer advanced either his moral or religious thought. He later gained the ear and procured the favor of presidents, but by the end of his twenty year career as an abolitionist his fire had

---

[70] Douglass, "The Prospect in the Future," *Douglass' Monthly*, August, 1860, 306–307.

faded. Douglass remained a nationally known figure for the duration of his life, but his characteristic passion lay largely dormant until it was revived near the end of his life by Ida B. Wells and the anti-lynching campaign. Stirred-on by battle, he rallied a final time.

5

CONCLUSION

From that time until now, I have been engaged in pleading the cause of my brethren with what success, and with what devotion, I leave those acquainted with my labors to decide.[1]

Frederick Douglass scholarship has documented his significance and contributions in myriad ways. Beyond this, and in ways that Douglass could not have imagined, scholars continue to investigate sources from which Douglass may have drawn in arriving at his own epistemology, and articulating his developing positions with respect to slavery and the other pressing social issues of his time. Students of Douglass's life work find traces of the intellectual currents of the day in the ideas that he defended on behalf of emancipation and elevation.

Two scholars in particular, intellectual biographers Waldo Martin and David Blight, offer fresh and compelling insights into Douglass's thought. Through their efforts, Douglass is recovered

---

[1] Frederick Douglass, *Narrative of the Life of Frederick Douglass, An American Slave, Written by Himself* (Boston: 1845), in Henry Louis Gates, Jr., ed. *Frederick Douglass/Autobiographies* (New York: Library of America/Penguin Books, 1994) 119.

as not only a rhetorician, but a thinker. This advance in understanding Douglass, however, raises some intriguing interpretive
questions. To what extent, if any, does intellectual biography
diminish its subject? And to what extent does it impede our own
efforts here at recovery? My concern is that contemporary intellectual biographers may inadvertently lose the inherent richness of
historic narrative accounts by focusing primarily on intellectual
currents.

While the task of locating Douglass within broader currents is
fruitful and necessary to understanding his mind, if it is done at the
expense of narrative, students of Douglass's life and work risk
missing, perhaps forever losing, the particularities, inconsistencies,
and tensions of his discrete existence. Can an intellectual
morphology of Frederick Douglass benefit from an emphasis on
his narrative? Will an emphasis on his narrative advance our
understanding of Douglass? I think so.

I propose to explore these questions by reviewing the
contributions of Martin and Blight, and by comparing them with
one biographer, Benjamin Quarles. For all their advances, Martin
and Blight lose something of Douglass that Quarles captures. They
lose the dialectical quality of Douglass's thought, and so the
process of contextual inquiry, critical reflection, and creative
response that issues in the mature formulations they consider.

For his part, James Hunt uses the learning and developmental
theories of Erik Erickson, Jean Piaget, Lawrence Kohlberg, and
James Fowler quite successfully to describe a process of change
and development in Douglass's faith journey. His characterization
of three major stages in Douglass's religious life (evangelical
Methodism, abolitionism, and religious liberalism) helps readers
to order and explain the broad shifts in religious awareness that
Douglass underwent. Hunt also does justice to the shift in
authority for Douglass's religious beliefs from the *say so* of trusted
others to granting legitimacy to the voice of a deeper self. Nevertheless, Hunt under-reports the lasting influences and continuities
of Douglass's evangelical and abolitionist past on his liberal
future. Douglass made commitments and discerned truths in those
early years that he maintained his entire life.

My narrative approach hopes to capture the best of both worlds. It treats the narrative as worthy of intellectual analysis, illumines the tensions that ensue from shifting convictions and commitments, and locates the narrative within broader philosophical currents that enrich Douglass's thought. It describes the changes that Douglass certainly underwent, while acknowledging the continuities that endured.[2]

The community of Douglass scholars was enriched immeasurably in 1984 when Waldo Martin published his seminal intellectual biography of Douglass. Writing the first such biography of Douglass, Martin succeeds in locating Douglass within the intellectual currents of the day. Insofar as it is possible to separate Nineteenth Century Euro-American and Afro-American thought, Martin finds traces of both in the Douglass corpus.

On the Euro-American side, Martin locates Douglass in the cross-currents of Enlightenment rationalism, romanticism, and Protestantism. On the Afro-American side, Douglass represents the predominant middle-class uplift ideology. More specifically, Douglass symbolizes the integrationist-assimilationist and protest approaches to Afro-American elevation.

Both sides of the spectrum coalesce in Douglass, exemplifying his "fundamental Americanism," providing an historical and intellectual canvass upon which Martin draws the interrelated categories of Douglass's thought. Martin paints four such categories with broad strokes. He identifies Douglass as a humanist, race advocate, social reformer, and public personality. A few words on each aspect are in order.

Martin writes in his preface that "the guiding assumption unifying Douglass's thought was an inveterate belief in a universal

---

[2] After engaging the work of Waldo Martin, David Blight, and Benjamin Quarles, I review my findings and comment on the effectiveness of my approach. I gratefully acknowledge the work of other scholars, such as John Blassingame, Philip Foner, Dickson Preston, Nathan Huggins, William Van DeBurg, and William McFeely, to name only a few. They have made valuable contributions to the field, and their work has enhanced my own.

and egalitarian brand of humanism."[3] Humanism, then, is the central concept in the mind of Douglass. He appealed to the conscience of America on behalf of its black population, and he devoted his life to the causes of emancipation, elevation, and social reform. Further, he demanded nothing for blacks that he did not also demand for all Americans. Pleas for freedom, institutional justice, and amity among blacks and whites were all consequences of Douglass's humanist bent.

Martin also cites Douglass's recognition of the fecundity of his experience as one of the basic categories of his thought. As Martin puts it, "Douglass's ability to illuminate major contemporary social and intellectual currents through the prism of his own experience characterized his intellectual odyssey."[4] As a result of this ability, Douglass provided readers with encyclopedic social commentary from a black perspective.

Notably absent from the basic categories is Douglass's religious thought. Though Martin does treat Douglass's religious thought, he is indebted to William Van Deburg's 1974 article, "Frederick Douglass: Maryland Slave to Religious Liberal." I want to record several reservations I have concerning the implications of Martin's treatment of Douglass's religious thought.

Martin asserts in his preface that Protestant Christianity provided Douglass with a "religious rationale for his deep-rooted moral sensibility."[5] If Protestant Christianity provided a religious basis, or fundamental reason for his moral sense, then abolitionism supplied the content of his religion. Martin states, in fact, that "abolitionism quickly assumed the status of a religion," for a youthful Douglass, "drawing upon the best Christian ideals: love, morality, and justice."[6] Martin writes: "Abolitionism, therefore, stood for more than the mere emancipation of his enslaved people; it also stood for the true religion. It was rational, or enlightened, as well as intuitive, or romantic. It exemplified the basically

---

[3] Waldo Martin, *The Mind of Frederick Douglass* (Chapel Hill: University of North Carolina Press, 1984) ix.

[4] Ibid., xi.

[5] Ibid., ix.

[6] Ibid., 20.

consistent Enlightenment and romantic notions of man's innate goodness."[7]

Martin here exposes several biases. First, he reduces Christianity to little more than an intellectual signpost and first cause in Douglass's thought, suggesting that abolition supplanted fideist religion as a surrogate.[8] Second, he grounds Douglass's thought, and Afro-American thought generally, in European and Euro-American thought without sufficiently demonstrating the intellectual contributions of the black experience. One comes away from Martin with the sense that Douglass's slave experience did little to promote his later intellectual formulations, or less than, say, Enlightenment rationalism and romanticism.

Christianity provided not only fertile soil for Douglass's thought but also the first harvest of important questions and ideas. Some of the ideas harvested from this soil survived the philosophical tempests that raged across his religious landscape in later years. At issue for interpreters of Douglass is the cost of emphasizing the philosophical discontinuities between his earlier religious convictions and later convictions, at the expense of convictional continuities. Abolition, for example, did not become Douglass's religion. Rather, abolition became Christian praxis. It did the work of "true" Christianity.

As a child, before Douglass knew what the word abolition meant, his religious epistemology took shape within a moral and religious belief system. Even at a young age, Douglass had the capacity to question the God of that system. Through inquiry into the truth of the matter and subsequent reflection on his experiences, Douglass concluded, contrary to teachings of the slaveholding church, that God intended for him to be free. His first Christian work was to free himself and, secondarily, to assist other slaves in gaining their freedom. Abolition became the primary mandate of Christian love and justice. Douglass knew at least this

---

[7] Ibid.

[8] James Hunt follows Martin here. "Abolitionist ideology became a surrogate religion, a new faith to replace the changing faith of his evangelical Methodism." James B. Hunt, "The Faith Journey of Frederick Douglass, 1818–1895," *Christian Scholar's Review*, 15:3, (March, 1986): 235.

much before his exposure to Garrisonian abolitionism and to natural rights philosophy.

On Martin's view, Douglass's youthful abolitionist religion shifted during the 1850s and 1860s to his mature religious liberalism. This process involved the demystification of religion, decreasing reliance upon divine determinism and increasing reliance upon human determination of human affairs.[9]

Accordingly, his conversion to religious liberalism pushed Douglass outside mainstream Nineteenth Century American Protestantism.[10] Martin writes that American Protestantism at the time (and especially black Protestantism) was notable for "a powerful sense of divine determinism in human affairs."[11] By Martin's account, Douglass came to realize the incompatibility of traditional Protestant Christianity with progressive social change. The "efforts of man himself," were more efficacious to the goal of social justice than the efforts "of an unseen and inscrutable God operating ambiguously and indirectly in human affairs through human conduct."[12]

By Martin's account, Douglass's conversion to religious liberalism was prompted by several factors, including: "early doubts concerning a proslavery and a prowhite God;" intellectual influences; and lastly, dreadful national decisions during the 1850s.[13] Those early doubts about God caused Douglass to lean away "from the sacred world view of his fellow slaves and toward a supremely rational view of man and the universe."[14]

As a corollary to this fundamental "leaning," Martin offers four intellectual influences that accelerated Douglass's conversion. Among them are: (1) Garrisonian criticism of the American Church and clergy; (2) belief in an evangelical religion stressing "good works" over the fine points of faith and metaphysics; (3) Theodore Parker's Transcendental Unitarianism and the liberalism

---

[9] Martin, *The Mind of Frederick Douglass*, 175.
[10] Ibid.
[11] Ibid.
[12] Ibid., 176.
[13] Ibid., 177–78.
[14] Ibid., 177.

of New England Unitarianism; and, (4) Douglass's thoroughgoing adherence to Enlightenment principles of natural law and rationality.

These influences, in conjunction with his prior skepticism, led Douglass to the brink of his conversion, but it was the tumultuous 1850s that sent Douglass over the edge and "signaled a watershed in his intellectual development."[15] Events like the Fugitive Slave Act, Kansas-Nebraska Act, and the Dred Scott ruling convinced Douglass that God's "direct involvement in human affairs was minimal."[16]

His conversion to religious liberalism complete, Douglass, in his capacity as social reformer, favored "the rationalism of positivism" over the "intuition of faith."[17] "Concrete human deeds" took precedence over "abstract prayers, miracles, and revelations."[18]

Though Martin understands Douglass's mature religious philosophy to be human-centered and not God-centered, he does not believe that Douglass jettisoned God altogether. Instead, Martin concludes:

> Even with God offstage, Douglass's social universe remained bound by a basic and tidy moral mechanism. Although he could no longer speak unequivocally on behalf of the power of Christian faith, prayer, and miracles, now he could speak unequivocally on behalf of a pragmatic religion... As shown in his mature religious and social reform philosophies, the basis of his characteristic optimism developed a more secular humanistic emphasis as compared to the more Christian and divine emphasis of his earlier optimism.[19]

---

[15] Ibid., 175.
[16] Ibid., 178.
[17] Ibid., 180.
[18] Ibid.
[19] Ibid.

In summary, terms that describe Martin's understanding of Douglass's mature religion include human-centered, secular humanistic, supremely rational, positivistic, pragmatic, and liberal. This reading fits well within the historical, intellectual matrix established by Martin at the outset. My approach, however, portrays a slightly different Douglass. While I acknowledge the same personal influences and philosophical trends that Martin raises in Douglass's thought, I seek out the perduring personal commitments, and religious and moral continuities disclosed in Douglass's narrative.

The upshot of this methodological difference is that I view the slave episode in Douglass's life as much more important to his mature thought than does Martin. Douglass's conceptions of divine providence and human agency, liberation and self-help, political reform and social justice, to name a few, were born in bondage and gave direction to Douglass's thought. Douglass did not need abolitionists to persuade him that slavery was anathema to God. He did not need Enlightenment thinkers to authorize the efficacy of concrete human deeds. He did not need German "freethinkers" to teach him that action, not angels, was the key to liberation. The slave who taught himself to read, resisted his overseer, plotted a failed escape attempt, and eventually succeeded in gaining his freedom, had a world view and a belief system before he ever read William Lloyd Garrison, Ralph Waldo Emerson, or Ludwig Feuerbach.

The ideological and philosophical currents of the day do not sufficiently explain Douglass's thought. They are necessary, but insufficient, to that end. They locate Douglass within an historical era, but are too universal to paint the fine lines and subtle hues that made Douglass a discrete thinker.

A narrative-dialectical approach roots Douglass's thought in a slave community on the eastern shore of Maryland in the early nineteenth century. Those roots fed moral convictions and religious commitments that Douglass either embraced, redacted, or jettisoned as he interpreted the ideological and philosophical ideas to which he was exposed. Early childhood experiences (e.g. not knowing his age or his father; being protected by a mother he hardly knew; being deceived into the life of a slave; etc.), for example, anticipate his characteristic self-reliance and restive spirit in a way that an appeal to broader intellectual currents cannot duplicate. Lessons learned under the individuals who populated Douglass's moral world imparted insights into Douglass's faith journey that are missed by an exclusive appeal to evangelical Methodism or to a "dependency" stage of moral development. Douglass learned by conviction, for example, that God had a great work for him to do. This conviction endured to the end of his life.

Like many Douglass scholars, Martin views a dramatic and fundamental shift in Douglass's thought during the 1850s. Where once Douglass advocated moral suasion and nonresistance, he subsequently advocated political action and even violence if necessary. Where once Douglass argued vociferously for the repeal of the Constitution and disunion, he subsequently claimed the Constitution and argued for continued national union. Where once Douglass was an African Methodist Episcopal Zion supply preacher, he subsequently despaired of clergy and of organized religion.

Martin attributes this shift, conversion, or about-face to the growing influence upon Douglass of the contemporary, intellectual currents, and to Douglass's adoption and application of those currents in response to the political setbacks of the 1850s. This is indeed a plausible reading of the evidence.

My use of narrative, however, suggests an alternate reading. Starting with the premise that we are born into an ongoing story and that we are comprised by stories, the goal of maturation is to gain a comprehensive understanding of ourselves, to create narrative unity and to affix meaning to our stories. To reach maturity, we edit our stories along the time line created by circumstance. We emphasize certain stories to the detriment of others, and we reconcile stories that exist in tension (e.g.: being black and being American). In short, we create a memory, and by so doing we define our truths and organize a discrete self. So it was with Douglass. Given the genealogical bias implicit in my approach, I look for antecedents during his early years in slavery to make sense of the changes described above. Next, I listen for any recognition of a conversion on Douglass's part. Then, I appeal to those who knew Douglass for recognition of change or conversion, and I hold those accounts in tension with what Douglass provides about his state of mind. Finally, I cross-reference this information with historical accounts.

Taking, for example, the shift from moral suasion to political action, I find more of an evolution or progression than a conversion or about-face. It was neither the intellectual currents of the day nor the political events of the day that made Douglass a proponent of political action and even violence. They inform when and how he changed, and even provide the language he used to explain his change. But they do not indicate why he changed.

The incident with the slave breaker, Covey, does more to explain why he changed than either a philosophical theory or a political event. Douglass changed from moral suasion to political action because doing so resolved a tension in the building narrative of his life.

The rebellious slave created a truth for himself in his defeat of Covey. He vowed that the white man who expected to succeed in whipping him would also have to succeed in killing him. Douglass remained true to this vow for the duration of his life, and it became one of the great principles or truths upon which he established his estimation of himself. The use of violence in defense against oppressive violence was morally permissible to Douglass at least as far back as the Covey episode.

When Douglass became a Garrisonian abolitionist and committed himself to nonresistance, another tension formed in his narrative. Nonresistance violated his prior commitment to the employment of physical force in opposition to physical force. For the duration of his tenure as a Garrisonian abolitionist, Douglass paid lip service to nonresistance, but he clearly could not abide by it.

It comes as no surprise that a formal, acknowledged shift to political action and defense of violence accompanied Douglass's break with the Garrisonians and linkage to Gerrit Smith and the Liberty Party. By throwing off the tenuously held commitment to Garrison's brand of abolition, Douglass was able to honor his prior fully engaged commitment, even within the parameters of Gerrit Smith's system.

A similar process can be discerned in Douglass's shift from what Martin calls a God-centered, traditional religion to a human-centered liberal religion. Scholars like Martin find a causal relationship between what they see as a growing secular humanist trend in Douglass's thought during the antebellum years and the influence of Enlightenment rationalism, American pragmatism and Transcendental Unitarianism. On this account, Douglass cast off his sacred world view and moved God offstage. Human moral agency, as opposed to divine moral agency, and pragmatic Christianity took center stage.

It is difficult to read Douglass without finding evidence of such a change. But when we inquire into the nature of the change, why it occurred, and why it occurred when it did, I believe an alternate reading of the evidence is possible. While it is true that Douglass did appeal to the Enlightenment views of the age and to the proliferation of rationalist arguments in the West, I believe that this reference does less finally to explain Douglass's mature religious thought than does the seeming futility of over twenty years work as a Christian abolitionist.

For better than two decades Douglass called upon fellow Christians to leave the slaveholding church, with no visible signs of success for that effort. The indifference he encountered among Christians to the gross injustice and evil of slavery led Douglass to believe that Negro hatred was "a part of American religion."[20] He further believed that only the direct intervention of God could cleanse the American conscience of its moral turpitude.

Though depressed and frustrated with the state of affairs in the 1850s, Douglass never pushed God offstage, nor did his religion become human-centered. Douglass believed consistently in the efficacy of human agency and divine providence. Unlike the Garrisonians, he never despaired of the church as an institution but lost hope in the ability of a sinful church to right itself. In a letter

---

[20] Philip Foner, ed. *The Life and Writings of Frederick Douglass* (New York: International Publishers, 1950) 2:502.

to the Secretary of the Edinburgh New Anti-Slavery Association
dated from 1857, Douglass expressed his religious sense:

> I am an apostate from Garrisonism—an "ism" which
> comprehends opposition to the Church, the ministry, the
> Sabbath and the government as institutions in themselves
> considered and viewed apart from the question of
> Slavery. I am opposed to them at these points and could
> not lend my humble influence to the spread of such
> opinions in the name of the Slave or his cause....I am now
> at work less under the influence of hope than the settled
> assurance of faith in God, and the ultimate triumph of
> righteousness in the world. The cause of the slave is a
> righteous one, and I believe precious in the sight of
> Heaven.[21]

Douglass did not lose faith in God, as this passage eloquently
testifies. He lost hope in the ability of the abolitionist movement to
free whites from slaveholding Christianity. Beyond this, he lost
hope in his ability to free blacks from an unthinking religion.
Douglass believed the black church needed reform as much as the
white church, but that does not mean that he was hostile to the
church as an institution. He was not. He was a Christian who was
thoroughly disgusted with the church in America. White Christians were largely unmoved by the harrowing testimonials coming
from slaves, and black Christians waited upon God to do that
which was in their own power to do, namely, liberate themselves.
Douglass ran out of confidence in the abolitionist movement and
the church in the antebellum years, but not out of faith in God.

Martin cites Douglass's self-reliance as further evidence of
his human-centered, secular religion. He suggests that the primacy
of human action in Douglass's thought is inconsistent with a
Christian emphasis on the primacy of divine action in human
affairs. For Martin, religion of the period is little more than a
philanthropic urge for the self-made individual. Martin writes:

---

[21] Ibid., 2:425–26.

"The nineteenth-century American ideals of self-improvement, material success, and the self-made man had a fiercely competitive economic basis, capitalism, as well as a related and paradoxical philanthropic basis, Protestantism."[22]

Though he is correct to ground Douglass in nineteenth-century American Protestantism, Martin tends to reduce the significance of Christianity for Douglass to a mere function. Did Douglass experience his religion on a paradoxical philanthropic basis? On the contrary, Christianity was something more for Douglass. It was more than merely the source of a work ethic. It was richer than merely a "supremely rational view of man and the universe."[23]

His religion in the antebellum years was sober, pragmatic, antiracist, and antisexist. Douglass wanted "true Christian civilization."[24] He even thought that the Christianization of Africa was a "desirable blessing."[25] My intention is not to suggest that Douglass possessed a thick sense of Christianity. My argument is that he did not reduce God to morality nor Christianity to philanthropy.

By way of conclusion, consider this passage from a letter to William Still, written in 1860, as evidence of my claims:

On the side of the oppressor there is power, now as in the earlier days of the world. I find much comfort in the thought that I am but a passenger on board of this ship of life. I have not the management committed to me. I am to obey orders, and leave the rest to the great Captain whose wisdom is able to direct. I have only to go on in His fear and in His spirit, uttering with pen and tongue the whole truth against Slavery, leaving to Him the honor and the glory of destroying this mighty work of the devil. I long for the end of my people's bondage, and would give all I possess to witness the great jubilee; but God can

---

[22] Martin, *The Mind of Frederick Douglass*, 255.
[23] Ibid., 177.
[24] Foner, *The Life and Writings of Frederick Douglass*, 2:448.
[25] Ibid., 2:443.

wait, and surely I may. If He, whose pure eyes cannot look upon sin with allowance, can permit the day of freedom to be deferred, I certainly can work and wait. The times are just now a little brighter; but I will walk by faith, not by sight, for all grounds of hope founded on external appearance, have thus far signally failed and broken down under me....Nevertheless, God reigns, and we need not despair, and I for one do not.[26]

David Blight joined the conversation on the mind of Douglass in 1989. Though less comprehensive than Martin's contribution, Blight presents the first attempt "to analyze the impact of the Civil War" in Douglass's "life and thought."[27] Blight makes reference to Martin's book, and by so doing, distinguishes his contribution from Martin's. "From Martin, we learn a great deal about Douglass's character and his world view, but not as much about how his ideas ebbed and flowed in response to events."[28] Blight, for his part, envisions a more accessible approach to Douglass's thought—one that captures the subtleties and nuances of particular existence.

Blight's work is less comprehensive in scope, more comprehensive in detailed understanding, and more attuned to the role of religion in Douglass's thought than that of Martin. Blight correctly perceives the significance of nineteenth century millennialism and apocalypticism as a shaping influence on Douglass. He writes: "Douglass saw the conflict [Civil War] in a spiritual framework. He interprets the slavery issue, secession, emancipation, and the war itself as a millennial nationalist. Through a combination of secular and religious ideas, Douglass made a major contribution to the apocalypticism with which his generation made sense out of the Civil War."[29]

---

[26] Ibid., 2:489.

[27] David Blight, *Frederick Douglass' Civil War* (Baton Rouge and London: Louisiana State University Press, 1989) xi.

[28] Ibid., xii.

[29] Ibid.

In fairness to Martin, he does acknowledge the influence of millennial thought, both religious and secular, on Douglass's philosophy of social reform.[30] But Blight provides a clearer analysis of how that influence shaped Douglass's thought.

Building upon Martin's work, Blight gives us more of what we need to know in order to locate Douglass's moral and religious sense. He provides the spiritual framework through which Douglass did indeed view the events of the day. But he does not yet give us the details, the specific content, of what he deems Douglass's "abiding religious faith."[31]

To understand Blight's explication of the spiritual framework he accords to Douglass, the reader must consider two indices of that framework, millennialism and apocalypticism. Noting that the companion concepts are fraught with ambiguity, Blight offers his working definitions of each. The essential chord of millennialism is God's Second Com-ing.[32] More specifically, nineteenth-century American millennial-ism is a

> cluster of religious and secular ideas inherited from the Puritans, refashioned through the Revolutionary era, nurtured through numerous waves of revivalism, and forged into a national creed during the antebellum period. It taught that Christ would have a Second Coming in the "new Israel" of America. Moreover, millennialism helped foster an American sense of mission, a belief that the United States was the "redeemer nation" destined to perform a special role in history.[33]

At the core of nineteenth-century American millennialist thought is the "expectation of God's extraordinary intervention in history to destroy an evil age and replace it with a new, eternal creation."[34]

---

[30] Martin, *The Mind of Frederick Douglass*, 173.
[31] Blight, *Frederick Douglass' Civil War*, 3.
[32] Ibid., 102.
[33] Ibid.
[34] Ibid., 104.

Ambiguity arises from the vagueness and paradox inherent in the concept. Millennialists proposed a Biblical vision of "dreadful calamity."[35] This pessimistic view of the millennium was often accompanied by an optimistic view of American perfectibility. "Prophecies of gloom and doom coexisted with ideas of national mission."[36] The upshot of this insight on millennialist ambiguity is that Douglass need not be understood as losing his faith in the 1850s. On the contrary, his vacillation between optimism and pessimism reflects the millennial tone of the period.

Apocalypticism, according to Blight's account, "was often a response to or an escape from the ambiguity in millennial expectation."[37] The paradox of a pessimistic future and an optimistic future is resolved in the religious belief that the present evil age will soon be overcome by the direct intervention of God, who will thereupon establish a new and everlasting age of righteousness.[38] Where Martin finds Douglass evolving from the sacred world view of "divine determinism" to the secular world view of "religious liberalism," Blight finds no such demystification and abandonment of the sacred.[39] Blight's correction is welcome. Martin does indeed "underestimate the significance of millennialism," in Douglass's mind. Douglass's assessment of human agency does not supersede his conception of divine omnipotence. As Blight indicates, the two were "equal forces" in much of nineteenth-century millennialist thought.

In addition to millennialism and apocalypticism, Blight argues that a doctrine of progress comprises the third index of Douglass's spiritual framework. This doctrine of progress, known alternately as meliorism, holds "that society has an innate tendency toward improvement and that this tendency may be furthered through conscious human effort."[40] If millennialism and

---

[35] Ibid.
[36] Ibid.
[37] Ibid.
[38] Ibid., 104.
[39] Ibid., 10.
[40] *The American Heritage Dictionary*, 3rd ed. (Boston: Houghton Mifflin Company, 1997) 848.

apocalypticism symbolize the work of divine omnipotence in Douglass's spiritual outlook, then meliorism symbolizes the work of human agency, work that complements and fulfills what God is doing in the world.

Progress to Douglass was "essentially moral and, ultimately, irrepressible."[41] As such, it was part of a providential theory of history.[42] This understanding of progress, rooted in providence, is inherently religious. The work of human agency may be secular, but even then it has a latent religious significance. Blight refers to this religious significance as "the idea of divine direction of human affairs."[43] Human agency is part of God's plan, and therefore will lead to God's kingdom. For this reason, progress invites optimism. It also explains why, even during his darkest hours in the mid-1850s, Douglass was able to wait "for the jubilee of black emancipation."[44]

Millennialism, progress, and apocalypticism comprise Douglass's "spiritual understanding of history," which is the framework through which he interpreted the events of the day.[45] Blight states: "Douglass arrived at this spiritual understanding of history...by less formal means than traditional theologians, but by the 1850s it had shaped his thinking and provided perhaps the deepest layer of his prewar hope."[46] Although Blight is not especially concerned with Douglass's religious thought *per se*, a reconstruction of the case he makes for Douglass's religious thought might appear as follows: Douglass was a moral determinist who rejected orthodoxy yet maintained an "abiding religious faith."[47]

Exposure to religious ideas as a child provided Douglass with confidence in the future and with sources of self-esteem, leading

---

[41] Blight, *Frederick Douglass' Civil War*, 6.
[42] Ibid.
[43] Ibid.
[44] Ibid., 9.
[45] Ibid.
[46] Ibid.
[47] Ibid., 3.

to a sense of personal destiny. His religious convictions "buoyed his spirit and molded his temperament."[48]

Beginning with his tenure as an abolitionist and for the rest of his life, Douglass assailed religious hypocrisy. He was as contemptuous of clergy as he was scornful of orthodoxy and dogma. During the 1840s and 1850s, as Douglass exhibited increasing political consciousness, his religious orientation changed as well. Douglass became more of a realist and opportunist. Accompanying this shift from principle to expediency in his political thinking was a growing reliance on reason and waning trust in revelation. Although he "preferred reason," Douglass "never gave up on revelation."[49] Blight is right. Douglass experienced a tension between reason and revelation—one that was not easily resolved by dropping either of the terms.

His wartime religious thought fits into the concurrent and overlapping theological traditions of millennialism, apocalypticism, civil religion, and the jeremiad. Like many other thinkers of his day, Douglass viewed the civil war as a rite of passage for the young nation. But more than this, he viewed the war as a cleansing tragedy of sorts and as a necessity for national atonement. Present suffering brought with it the promise of future regeneration. A new nation under God was the underlying hope of his fervor.

Blight advances Martin's account in several respects. Generally, he does indeed provide readers with more of an "ebb and flow of ideas to events" in Douglass's life. More specifically, he provides a religious framework that is essential to understanding the mind of Douglass. By so doing, he presents a more complex and accurate picture of Douglass's religious thought. Further, Blight is more apt than Martin to concede tensions and contradictions in Douglass.

For all his accomplishments, I believe that Blight shares an interpretive approach with Martin that leads him to under-report on Douglass as a discrete thinker. Concepts such as millennialism,

---

[48] Ibid., 7.
[49] Ibid., 120.

apocalypticism, and progress do much to locate Douglass within a religious milieu, but do not enable us to distinguish Douglass from other religious thinkers of the period. Further, methods that rely exclusively upon these concepts treat only mature formulations of thought at the expense of very fruitful antecedents. In this regard, they tend to be incomplete. These methods are useful hermeneutical tools, functioning much like intellectual plumb lines. But they are ultimately not sufficient. They do not go far enough, or delve deep enough, to explain why Douglass developed and thought as he did. As a consequence of this limitation, intellectual biographers can underestimate the significance of religion in Douglass's life, the significance of the slave episode in fashioning Douglass's religious thought, and the complexity of his religious thought.

Interestingly, biographer Benjamin Quarles does better at explaining Douglass's religious views, even without a formal appeal to the intellectual trends that characterized Douglass's religious milieu. He appeals to Douglass's autobiographies and to the testimony of contemporaries for an understanding of Douglass's moral and religious thought:

> Douglass' coolness to organized religion sprang in part from the "otherworldliness" of much that went on in the Negro church. Himself a militant, ever braced to "take arms against a sea of troubles," Douglass held that too many Negro clergymen preached a gospel of resignation, of passiveness, of being so preoccupied with the city called heaven that they did not rebel against the status quo here below. To Douglass religion should have been an instrument for social reconstruction; instead it was largely, he felt, the chief stock in trade of a theologically-untrained and "folksy" clergy who used it as a device for making the underprivileged Negro forget social reality by fixing his eyes on a distant land of milk and honey to be

reached by prayerfully waiting for the chariot to swing low.[50]

The charge of "otherworldliness" is antiquated. The Negro church was no more otherworldly than white churches that preached the kingdom of God. This dated reference notwithstanding, Quarles is correct in maintaining that Douglass disavowed the "passive" nature of the Negro church.

By appealing to Douglass's narrative to help explain his mature view of the Negro church, Quarles adds vital information to the intellectual overview of Martin and Blight. The former slave who freed himself was not completely comfortable with what he understood to be a slave church. Nor was he satisfied with the slaveholding church. He did not favor the total absence of the church as an institution, as was the Garrisonian position on the matter. In the middle nineteenth century, he did not have many other options. Douglass flirted with Transcendental Unitarianism and returned sporadically to the African Methodist Episcopal Church. He enjoyed the "higher criticism" of the former and the passion and familiarity of the latter.

During his early years as a slave, "he went down on his knees regularly." But it was not, Quarles writes, until he "prayed with his heels" that he became free.[51] Quarles not only captures Douglass's fighting spirit but also a fundamental religious conviction (God helps those who help themselves), and moral commitment (self-help). To know Douglass, we must know that he "prayed with his heels," and that this prayer was not godless. We must also know that he believed: "All the prayers of Christendom cannot stop the force of a single bullet, divert arsenic of its poison, or suspend any law of nature."[52] Consider these quotes as evidence of Douglass the deist, perhaps, or Douglass the child of Enlightenment Rationalism. The problem is that to know Douglass we must also

---

[50] Benjamin Quarles, *Frederick Douglass* (New York: Atheneum, 1968) 295.

[51] Benjamin Quarles, *Frederick Douglass*, (New York: Da Capo Press, Inc., reprint 1997) 295.

[52] Ibid.

know that the man who held these beliefs was one who sang "In Thy Cleft, Oh, Rock of Ages;"[53] who expressed feeling "thrilled" to hear a Methodist pastor sing "Jesus my Savior, to Bethlehem came, Seeking for me; for me;"[54] and who was quoted as saying to Rev. Henry Ward Beecher in 1850 "Now I am in the trade winds of the Almighty."[55] Consider these quotes as evidence of a more evangelical Douglass. To know Douglass we must see the tension of holding both accounts together, scripture and common sense, and refuse to resolve the tension.

Concepts like "religious liberalism" and "free religionist" express a commitment to spiritual and religious liberty, and help to explain why religious thinkers like Douglass did not have a favorable view of the traditional church. These terms denote some theological commitments and religious sensibilities that Douglass shared with fellow New England abolitionists. But "religious liberalism" as a concept does not explain sufficiently why Douglass, as a discrete moral agent, was displeased with the church. One must scour his narrative for that answer. His displeasure had more to do with his anger at the hypocrisy of the church and his judgments about the role of the church in the emancipation and elevation of black people than with formalized philosophical or theological positions.

Douglass believed that the Negro church and the slaveholding church were both morally culpable for the continuation of slavery. With no covenant community of like-minded believers, Douglass remained outside the church and openly critical of it for the better part of his life. His praise for liberation from slavery and for the elevation of African Americans by the dint of human effort precipitated the charge of apostasy leveled at him from black and white clergy.

Douglass did not attack Christianity or organized religion *per se*, but he took the church to task for several failings. First, he was

---

[53] Interview with Francis J. Grimke, *Washington* (DC) *Evening Star*, February 22, 1895.

[54] Rev. J. T. Jenifer, *In Memoriam: Frederick Douglass* (Freeport NY: Books for Libraries Press, 1971, 1897) 27–28.

[55] Ibid., 27.

critical of the church when it promoted or sanctioned a composite of love for God and hatred of blacks. Second, he was critical when it exorcised freedom of thought as an act of apostasy and blessed only uncritical or unreasoning zeal. Third, he was critical when the church aligned itself with powerful money interests and concealed its worldly compromises under a shroud of spiritual authority. Given the social practices of the church during his lifetime, Douglass took the church to task for these and other failings quite often.

Douglass also supported the church. Though he claimed no particular denominational affiliation in his senior years, he contributed financially to individual congregations. Douglass held that the church was in a position to promote honorable character and conduct. He believed that on the whole churches contributed "to the improvement and moral elevation of those who came within the reach of their influence." Although not a regular churchgoer, Douglass did not go out of his way to socialize with the ungodly. He numbered several prominent clergymen among his closest acquaintances. Douglass was a Christian who expressed his trust in the Christian God, if not in the American church.[56]

Though he views Douglass as a free religionist, Quarles acknowledges that Douglass had some continuing interest in the African Methodist Episcopal Church during his later years. His interest was genuine indeed, as attested to in memoriam: "As he grew older he became possessed by a conviction of salvation. 'I have no uneasiness about the hereafter,' he was heard to say in later years, 'I am in the tradewinds of God. My back was launched by him, and he is taking it into port.'" The Reverend J. T. Jenifer related that "several times within a few months" before his death, Douglass expressed to him the joy he experienced in God and in spiritual life. In his later years Douglass occasionally attended Jenifer's church, the Metropolitan AME Church.[57]

---

[56] Benjamin Quarles, *Frederick Dougalss* (New York: Da Capo Press, 1997 [orig. Associated Publishers, 1948]) 296–97.
[57] Quarles, *Frederick Dougalss*, 297.

It is significant that Douglass did not jettison Christianity or religion altogether. It is also significant that he maintained some sporadic contact with the AME Church. Given his troubled relationship with the church, Douglass was most at home in a Christian church that was rooted in the black tradition; and in one that did not lend itself either to excessive religious zeal or to socio-political obsequiousness. Worship was a sober affair for Douglass, and one that lent itself to the mental, moral, and spiritual improvement of worshipers. Dickson Preston recounts that Douglass, while still a slave in Baltimore, left the Bethel African Methodist Church for the Sharp Street AME Church when five of Bethel's trustees signed an open letter denouncing the efforts of northern abolitionists as dangerous to free blacks as well as slaves.[58]

Douglass's convictions are most clearly revealed in stories. These stories delineate his social location, providing readers with moral and religious antecedents that are necessary for a more complete understanding. The stories of his mother and grandmother, for example, provide insights into Douglass's moral development that can go unappreciated or under-appreciated by biographers who utilize non-narrative theories to make sense of Douglass. More than a marginal historical reference, the women who loved the young Douglass contributed immeasurably to his self-awareness and self-esteem.

Maternal love, however, is insufficient to explain the rise of the anomalous Douglass. The fact that Douglass was a slave on the Eastern Shore of Maryland during a period of economic decline in the early nineteenth-century-owned by a master who favored him above other slave children—cannot be taken for granted. The circumstances into which Douglass was born afforded him the psychological space necessary for moral reflection. Though he remained on the Lloyd Plantation for only a year and a half, the special circumstances of his servitude allowed Douglass to become an outside observer. He viewed slavery and the relationship

---

[58] Dickson Preston, *Young Frederick Douglass: The Maryland Years* (Baltimore: Johns Hopkins University Press, 1980) 149–50.

of blacks and whites from a perspective that was peculiarly his own. The socio-economic circumstances surrounding his birth and formative years provide more than marginal historical points of reference.

During the slave episode he formed an understanding of God, the God of the Bible as preached in slave religion, that supported his desire for freedom. His exposure to abolitionist ideology, through the *Columbian Orator* gave him critical leverage against slavery and a linguistic currency, but the desire to be free is a feature of every human life. Douglass incorporated his abolitionist learnings within a vibrant, if embryonic, Christian faith that infused human agency with divine power.

Illustrative of Douglass's approach to religion during this episode was his approach to the Sabbath school he conducted for fellow slaves. With estimates running from twenty to forty "scholars," the school is memorable for the escape plan it harbored. Douglass's school was not merely a cover for the failed escape attempt. Douglass intended to free only himself at first, but was so impressed by several of those who attended the school that he included them in his plot. Those who impressed him demonstrated character ("manhood"). They risked thirty-nine lashes to attend the school, and their very lives if they failed to escape. In his later autobiographical accounts, Douglass expressed remorse about the fate of those brave men. They were special to Douglass because they had courage in addition to faith. They believed, like Douglass, that it was up to the slave to liberate herself. This was true Christianity in practice for Douglass.

Though he never participated in a violent revolt, Douglass believed that the use of violence by slaves against slaveholders and their agents was morally justifiable as self-defense against kidnappers. It is not at all clear, however, that Douglass held this belief without tension. One cannot imagine Douglass at any time in his life truly believing that he would have been justified in killing Lucretia Auld, or Hugh and Sophia Auld to liberate himself. Like Lucretia Auld, Hugh and Sophia were slaveholders, and therefore enemies, but they were also exceptions in Douglass's mind. Sophia Auld especially was a significant mother figure in Douglass's development. As a general principle, Douglass defends the use of lethal force in resisting slavery, but he neither advocated nor participated in pre-emptive attacks.

I began this study by indicating that I would attempt to trace the interplay of circumstances imposed and decisions made within a narrative framework. I find that a narrative-dialectical approach to the life and thought of Douglass illumines this interplay distinctively. It prevents us on the one side from trying to isolate his mind from its social location, from the experiences that generated his thought. I have sought to examine this location and those experiences both on the large scale of the social and cultural circumstances of his epoch and on the personal scale of identifiable episodes in his life. We have seen, for example, that he benefited from circumstantial luck.

A narrative approach prevents us on the other side from simply dissolving the agential *I* into the social *me*. I have described Douglass as an irreducible agent, who played an active rather than a passive role in the formation and development of his own character, who made choices and shaped his pilgrimage where in the outcomes were not all foregone conclusions. Even his emerging moral and religious views, including his use of Bible and his appropriation of the views of the overall abolitionist movement, show an independent agent in action. Douglass did more than simply reflect the ideas of others; he selected, revised, and transformed the episodes and intellectual currents that impinged upon him, and gained his own distinct integrity in the process. The resulting character, displayed peculiarly well by narrative analysis, yields a particular life as lived in all its complexities, its tensions and inconsistencies. Narrative is not system-building, nor does it format individuals, and thereby speak for them. On the contrary, narrative allows individuals to speak for themselves. It depicts "thick" personhood, never abstracted from its social matrix, but also never thoroughly a preordained product of social forces.

Yet this narrative approach carries an important limitation. It stays close to the character it serves to render. This closeness tempts researchers to introduce other interpretive vantage points and comparisons, especially at those points where the narrative is "thin," uncertain or unclear. I have tried to resist this temptation, to import as little as possible, to privilege what Douglass privileged, to base my understanding and substantiate my judgments from within his own corpus. Where his account is thin, my account is thin. I have tempted to restrain my judgments, using them to make connections between ideas and events in Douglass's life. Studies that strive to reach more ambitious comparative conclusions are doubtless legitimate and important. Yet I believe that the sort of close attention to narrative details that I have endeavored to provide furnishes one indispensable starting point for wider inquiries, attention that cuts down on the risk that we mask our conclusions in the guise of the subject's convictions. The convictions in this case remain too significant to allow that infraction, wittingly or unwittingly, to happen. The religious and moral thought I have canvassed, embedded in narrated life, has permanent lessons to teach within the limits this narrative imposes.

SELECTED BIBLIOGRAPHY

I list only the writings that have been of use in the making of this dissertation. This bibliography is by no means a complete record of all the works and sources I have consulted. It indicates the substance and range of reading upon which I have formed my ideas, and I intend it to serve as a convenience for those who wish to pursue the study of Frederick Douglass by utilizing the insights of literary theory, narrative ethics, and American history.

1. ARCHIVES

Yale University Library, New Haven, Connecticut. The James Weldon Johnson Collection.

2. WRITINGS OF FREDERICK DOUGLASS

Autobiographies
Douglass, Frederick. *Life and Times of Frederick Douglass*. Hartford CT: Park Publishing Company, 1881.
Gates, Henry Louis, Jr., editor. *Frederick Douglass/Autobiographies*: *My Bondage and My Freedom* (New York, 1855). New York: Library of America/Penguin Books, 1994.

————. *Frederick Douglass/Autobiographies*: *Narrative of the Life of Frederick Douglass, An American Slave, Written by Himself* (Boston, 1845). New York: Library of America/Penguin Books, 1994.
————. *Frederick Douglass/Autobiographies*: *Life and Times of Frederick Douglass* (Boston, 1893). New York: Library of America/Penguin Books, 1994.

Journals
North Star (Rochester NY), 1847–1851.
Frederick Douglass' Paper (Rochester NY), 1851–1860.
Douglass' Monthly (Rochester NY), 1859–1863.
Novella
Douglass, Frederick. "The Heroic Slave." In *Three Classic African-American Novels*, edited by William L. Andrews. New York: Penguin Books, 1990.

3. NEWSPAPERS AND PERIODICALS

The New York Times, 1895.
The Liberator (Boston), 1845–1865.
Evening Star (Washington DC), 1895.

4. LITERARY THEORY AND AFRICAN-AMERICAN LITERARY THEORY

Davis, Charles T. and Henry Louis Gates, Jr. *The Slave's Narrative*. Oxford: Oxford University Press, 1985.
Gibson, Donald B., "Christianity and Individualism: (Re-)Creation and Reality in Frederick Douglass's Representation of Self." *African-American Review* 26/4 (1992): 591–601.
Hubbard, Dolan. ."..Ah said ah'd save de text for you: Recontextualizing the Sermon to Tell (Her) Story in Zora Neale Hurston's 'Their Eyes Were Watching God'." *African-American Review* 27/ 2 (1993): 167.

Kermode, Frank. *The Sense of an Ending: Studies in the Theory of Fiction*. New York: Oxford University Press, 1967.

Leitch, Thomas M. *What Stories Are: Narrative Theory and Interpretation*. University Park: Pennsylvania State University Press, 1986.

Smith, Barbara H. "Narrative Versions, Narrative Theories." In *American Criticism in the Poststructuralist Age*, edited by Ira Konisberg, 162–86. Ann Arbor: University of Michigan, 1981.

5. ETHICS, SOCIOLOGY, AND THEOLOGY

Allen, Richard C. "When Narrative Fails." *Journal of Religious Ethics* 21/1 (1993): 27–68.

Cortese, Anthony. *Ethnic Ethics: The Restructuring of Moral Theory*. Albany: State University of New York Press, 1990.

Crites, Stephen. "The Narrative Quality of Experience." *Journal of the American Academy of Religion* 39 (1971): 292–311.

Frei, Hans. *The Eclipse of Biblical Narrative*. New Haven: Yale University Press, 1974.

Hauerwas, Stanley. *A Community of Character*. Notre Dame: University of Notre Dame Press, 1981.

———. *The Peaceable Kingdom*. Notre Dame: University of Notre Dame Press, 1983.

Kelsey, David. *The Uses of Scripture in Recent Theology*. Philadelphia: Fortress Press, 1975.

Kerby, Anthony. *Narrative and the Self*. Bloomington: Indiana University Press, 1991.

Lindbeck, George. *The Nature of Doctrine*. Philadelphia: Westminster Press, 1984.

Livingston, James. *Anatomy of the Sacred: An Introduction to Religion*. New York: Macmillan Publishing Company, 1989.

MacIntyre, Alasdair. *After Virtue*. Notre Dame: University of Notre Dame Press, 1981.

Meilaender, Gilbert C. *The Theory and Practice of Virtue*. Notre Dame: University of Notre Dame Press, 1984.

Nelson, Paul. *Narrative and Morality: A Theological Inquiry*. University Park: Pennsylvania State University Press, 1987.

Ogletree, Thomas. "Character and Narrative: Stanley Hauerwas' Studies of the Christian Life." *Religious Studies Review* 6/1 (1980): 26–29.

Outka, Gene. "Character, Vision and Narrative." *Religious Studies Review* 6/1 (1980): 110–18.

Placher, William. *Unapologetic Theology*. Louisville: John Knox Press, 1989.

Robbins, J. Wesley. "Narrative, Morality and Religion." *Journal of Religious Ethics* 8 (1980): 161–76.

6. AMERICAN HISTORY, RELIGION, AND BIOGRAPHY

Bennett, Lerone, Jr. *Before the Mayflower: A History of Black America*. 1962. Reprint, New York: Penguin Books, 1993.

Bingham, Caleb. "The Columbian Orator" [Boston, 1797]. In *The Columbian Orator*, edited by Val J. Halamandaris, 186–88. Washington DC: Caring Publications, 1997.

Blassingame, John W., et al., editors. *The Frederick Douglass Papers*. 5 volumes. New Haven: Yale University Press, 1979.

Blight, David. *Frederick Douglass' Civil War*. Baton Rouge: Louisiana State University Press, 1989.

Coppin, L. J. *Unwritten History*. 1919. Reprint, New York: Negro Universities Press, 1968.

Davis, Noah. *A Narrative of the Life of Reverend Noah Davis, A Colored Man*. James Weldon Johnson Collection. Yale University Library. Baltimore: J. F. Weishampel, Jr., 1859.

Fields, Barbara. *Slavery and Freedom on the Middle Ground: Maryland During the Nineteenth Century*. New Haven: Yale University Press, 1985.

Foner, Philip. *The Life and Writings of Frederick Douglass*. New York: International Publishers, 1950.

Franklin, John H. and Alfred A. Moss. *From Slavery to Freedom: A History of Negro Americans*. 1947. Reprint, New York: McGraw-Hill, Inc., 1988.

Fredrickson, George. *The Inner Civil War*. New York: Harper and Row, 1965.

Frothingham, Octavius B. *Transcendentalism in New England: A History*. 1876. Reprint, Philadelphia: University of Pennsylvania Press, 1972.

Green, William. *Narrative of Events In the Life of William Green, Formerly a Slave.*Springfield MO: L. M. Guernsey, 1853. James Weldon Johnson Collection. Yale University Library.

Huggins, Nathan I. *Slave and Citizen: the Life of Frederick Douglass*. Boston: Little, Brown and Company, 1980.

Jenifer, Reverend J. T. *In Memoriam: Frederick Douglass*. Freeport NY: Books for Libraries Press, 1971.

Kolchin, Peter. *American Slavery: 1619–1877*. New York: Hill and Wang, 1993.

Lewis, David L., editor. *W. E. B. DuBois: A Reader*. New York: Henry Holt and Company, 1995.

Martin, Waldo. *The Mind of Frederick Douglass*. Chapel Hill: University of North Carolina Press, 1984.

Meier, August. *Negro Thought in America: 1880–1915*. Ann Arbor: University of Michigan Press, 1963.

Solomon Northup, *Twelve Years A Slave. Narrative of Solomon Northup, A Citizen of New York, Kidnaped in Washington City in 1841, and Rescued in 1853, From a Cotton Plantation Near the Red River, in Louisiana*. 1853. In *A Documentary History of Slavery in North America* edited by Willie Lee Rose, 307–15. New York: Oxford University Press, 1976.

Pease, William and Jane Pease, editors. *The Antislavery Argument*. New York: The Bobbs-Merrill Company, 1965.

Preston, Dickson. *Young Frederick Douglass: The Maryland Years*. Baltimore: Johns Hopkins University Press, 1980.

Quarles, Benjamin. *Frederick Douglass*. New York: Atheneum, 1968.

Raboteau, Albert J. *Slave Religion*. New York: Oxford University Press, 1978.

Rose, Willie Lee, editor. *A Documentary History of Slavery in North America*. New York: Oxford University Press, 1976.

Stampp, Kenneth. *The Peculiar Institution*. 1956. Reprint, New York: Vintage Books, 1989.

Steward, Austin. *22 Years a Slave and 40 Years a Freeman*. 1857. Reprint, Massachusetts: Addison-Wesley Company, 1969.

Van Deburg, William L. "Frederick Douglass: Maryland Slave to Religious Liberal." *Maryland Historical Magazine* 69 (Spring 1974): 27–43.

Walker, David. *David Walker's Appeal*. 1829. Reprint, New York: Hill and Wang, 1965.

Warren, Austin. *The New England Conscience*. Ann Arbor: University of Michigan Press, 1966.

Williams, James. *Life and Adventures of James Williams, A Fugitive Slave, With a Full Description of the Underground Railroad*. San Francisco: Women's Union Print, 1873. James Weldon Johnson Collection. Yale University Library.

Wilmore, Gayraud S. *Black Religion and Black Radicalism*. 1973. Reprint, New York: Orbis Books, 1994.

ACKNOWLEDGMENTS

I cannot say that it takes a village to raise a child, I have not tried. But it has certainly taken a village to complete this study. I am in debt to a great many people, and I fear that I can no longer name all the people to whom I am indebted. Still, I am very grateful for all the technical assistance and encouragement I have received while engaged in this project. It is fitting that my last words here are words of thanks.

My parents, Clarence and Odella Williamson, and my sister, Rachel Lynn, celebrated every success along the way and did not let me dwell too long on the dark side when those successes were followed by setbacks. I owe my interest in narrative to them. My parents taught me much about life by telling stories. I remember my father telling me, while tossing the football, that the art of living is a lot like the art of fighting fires: you just have to get in there to see what you've got because appearances from the "outside" are often deceptive. My approach to Frederick Douglass is grounded in that orientation. My mother has been a role model for me as well. She began her M.Div. studies at Drew Theological Seminary the year before I began my studies at Yale Divinity School. Needless to say, she was a far better student than her son. Among her many talents, my mother keeps the family stories and recipes alive. The past comes to life in her sparkling eyes and through her words, and I know that my sacred cosmos is richly populated. A word of thanks goes to my sister as well. Now that the childhood trauma of growing up with a big sister is healed, I appreciate in new ways her commitments to family. Perhaps one day I will write an article entitled "Big Sister Ethics" in her honor.

I have another family to thank as well. The Reverend Dr. Robert O. Stuart was chaplain at my alma mater, Bates College, at a time when I was searching for direction. Along with his wife, the Reverend Lorna

Stuart and family, Rob encouraged me to think seriously about graduate school in ethics. His encouragement led to not only graduate school, but to ministry as well.

My dissertation directors, Gene Outka and John Blassingame read far too many rough drafts. The experience of crafting a dissertation under the supervision of such distinguished scholars is one for which I am very grateful. Trying to please an ethicist and a historian was not always a pleasant endeavor, but it was consistently challenging and entirely rewarding.

Several colleagues at Louisville Presbyterian Theological Seminary helped me in editing this project. I am particularly indebted to Melissa Nebelsick, Cauleen Spatz, and Cristol Kleitz. Finally, one of my students, Keith Click, was able to order the revised *Columbian Orator* for me. I was pleasantly surprised to learn that a revised edition was published in 1997.

Perhaps my greatest debt is to several friends who made sure that I did not become a recluse while engaged in the early stages of research and writing. Cheryl Jansen called me each day to make sure that I was writing when I needed to be writing, and playing when I needed to be playing. Kersten Raccio enlightened me regarding the medicinal benefits of a good bowl of pasta, red wine, and Italian pastry.

My "boyz," Stephen Ray and Dale Andrews, helped me to keep an even keel in troubled waters. Gordon Marino helped me to keep my eyes on the prize. My "little brother" Jared has been a source of inspiration and a great movie buddy. A word of thanks as well to a dear friend who did not live to see me complete this project. Here's to you, Olu.

Finally, I owe a debt to the Fern Creek Fire Department. They accepted me not only as a fellow volunteer fire fighter, but also as a brother. I fondly remembered the laughs we shared while I was in the throes of editing. Here's to chief Schmidt and Fern Creek's bravest. Thanks especially to Ron Renner, J. R. and Brandie Ayers, Josh and Rebecca White, Kyle Adams, Chad Ledington, Ken Nichter, Rob Davis, Steve Lobue, James Vandenbos, and Jeff Schank. I am honored to keep company with these men and women.

This is my village. They made this project possible. I, of course, assume all responsibility for the limitations that remain.

INDEX